The Dai

MW01233826

Ketogenic Diet

Cookbook

Restoring Your Health and Wellness Using a

Nutritional Approach with Over 200 Dairy-free

Ketogenic Recipes

By Helen Min

Table of Contents

Introduction

Firstly, I congratulate you for getting a copy of this piece. The Ketogenic diet has now become well known for losing weight through a strange phenomenon. It is called strange because for some people depending upon fats for losing fats sounds astonishing! We cannot normally imagine that we have to eat the same thing that we want to eliminate from our body - fats! The Ketogenic diet consists of high amounts of fats, ample proteins and fewer carbohydrates.

Not including dairy from your diet can be an effective way to speed up your weight loss and help reversing type 2 diabetes. Dairy products contain not only milk sugar (lactose), but also milk protein (casein), which stimulates insulin secretion more than other types of protein.

Doesn't it seem like dairy is in everything? From keto recipes to high-carb snacks and candy, there's some kind of milk product in so many things that we eat.

This isn't a problem if you're not allergic or intolerant to dairy at all, but what should you do if struggle with lactose or dairy proteins — especially when you are on a diet that typically consists of a lot of dairy like the ketogenic diet?

In addition to tantalizing your palate with tasty recipes, Dairy-Free Keto Cooking will teach you how to restore your health and wellness, while living a lifestyle that nourishes you in mind, body, and spirit. Whether your goal is to lose weight, heal your body from the inside out, or simply find your own personal version of food freedom, this book will help you along in your journey to finding your personal path to wellness.

This book contains everything you need to know about Dairy free and keto diets with over 200 dairy free ketogenic recipes for restoring health and wellness.

Chapter One: Introduction to Keto

What is the Ketogenic Diet?

You might have heard your friends talking about ketosis, the Ketogenic diet, etc. And, here you are researching about what they are talking about so passionately. The Ketogenic diet has now become well known for losing weight through a strange phenomenon. It is called strange because for some people depending upon fats for losing fats sounds astonishing! We cannot normally imagine that we have to eat the same thing that we want to eliminate from our body - fats! The Ketogenic diet consists of high amounts of fats, ample proteins and fewer carbohydrates. It forces the body to use fats instead of carbs for breaking down to convert them into energy. In our regular diets, we consume more carbohydrate and shun fats. Thus, our body is perfectly adapted throughout history to break down carbohydrates for energy. However, in the Ketogenic diet, we try to change the pattern of our body to break down the elements to be used for energy. We feed our body with more fats and less carbohydrates and thus force it to adapt in a new way to use fats for energy.

The plus side to this diet is that you do not have to count your calories or the amount of fats you are consuming like the way you do in other diets. You can indulge in different types of meats and oils, do not feel guilty and still lose weight. Normally, our body would convert food into glucose that would be transported to various body parts. This glucose is especially important in fueling functions of the brain. It is easiest for your body to convert carbs into glucose and use it as energy. Thus, it is obvious that your body will choose carbs over any other source of energy. Our body produces insulin to process glucose in the bloodstream and makes it travel around the body. Since glucose is there to provide energy to your body, fats are not required and hence, stored.

However, if you do not feed your body with carbohydrates, the liver starts converting fats to ketone bodies and fatty acids. These ketone bodies enter the brain and pass through it to replace the old source of energy, which was glucose. Thus, all the fats you consume in the form of meats, oils, creams, etc. is broken down and it does not get accumulated in your body.

When you lower down the carbs intake, the body is persuaded to enter into a state of ketosis. It is just a natural process, which is initiated by the body to help it survive when the food consumption is low. The Ketogenic diet is known by some other names as well- low carbs high fat diet (LCHF), low carb diet. The ultimate aim of a well-maintained Ketogenic diet is to persuade the body into a metabolic state. But this does not mean that you have to go hungry on calories. However, you just have to strictly control your consumption of carbohydrates. It is definitely easier than starving on fats. Human body is extremely adaptive to everything it is forced into. If you make it depend on a new source of energy rather than the regular one, it will adapt accordingly in a few days.

How to Lose Weight with the Ketogenic Diet?

The following tips should be applied while losing weight through the ketogenic diet plan:

1. Choose a diet containing fewer carbohydrates

You need to cut down on your consumption of starch and sugar. This idea is more than a century old. There have been a lot of diet plans which are based on reducing the amount of carbs you take. The new thing with the Ketogenic diet is that you provide your body with an alternate source of energy to depend on, which is fats. When you do not eat carbohydrates or eat them moderately, your body is capable of burning 300 additional calories per day, even when you are resting! It means that this amount of burnt calories is equal to a gym session of moderate physical activity.

2. Eat when you feel hungry

You do not need to stay hungry all the time to lose weight. This is the most common mistake committed by people who start a low carb diet. In the Ketogenic diet, you do not have to be scared of fats. Carbohydrates and fats are two major sources of energy for our body. If you are snatching carbs from your body, you need to give it an ample supply of fats. Low fats and low carbs equal to starvation, and we do not want that, do we? Starvation results in cravings and fatigue. That is why, people who starve give up easily on their diet plans. The better solution is to consume natural fat till the time you are satisfied. Some of the natural fats are full fat cream, butter, olive oil, meat, bacon, fatty fish, coconut oil, eggs.

3. **Eat real food**

This is one more common mistake made by Ketogenic followers that they get fooled by the fraudulent but creative marketing of "low-carb" foods. A real Ketogenic diet should be supported by real food. It implies the food which is being eaten by humans for millions of years. For example, fish, meat, vegetables, olive oil, butter, nuts, etc.

4. **Eat only if you feel hungry**

You must have read tip number 2 above. In the Ketogenic diet, eat when you are hungry. Do not eat when you are not feeling hungry. Let us elaborate why we are stressing this point again. Unnecessary snacking may become a mammoth issue in the Ketogenic diet. Some products are just so easily available, and they are so tempting that you cannot resist them.

5. **You can skip meals**

Yes, you heard it right. You can even skip breakfast if you are not feeling hungry. This holds truth for any meal. When you are strictly following the Ketogenic diet, your hunger goes down significantly, especially if you have to lose a lot of weight. Your body is happily busy in burning excess fats and reduces your temptation to eat.

6. **Wisely measure your development**

Losing weight successfully might get trickier sometimes. If you focus on your weight all the time and step on the weighing scale all the time, you may get mislead. It de-motivates you and makes you anxious needlessly.

7. **Be persistent**

You would have all those chunks of fats around your waist and thighs in several years. So, how do you expect to lose all the extra fat in just a few weeks? If you want to shed that extra weight permanently, you have to make persistent efforts.

What Is the Difference Between Dairy-Free Keto and Paleo?

The paleo diet is an eating plan based on what prehistoric humans might have eaten. It eliminates grains, legumes, processed sugar, and most dairy sources, but lets you eat meats, eggs, nuts and seeds, fruits, vegetables, unrefined fats and oils, and natural sweeteners (such as maple syrup and honey). Although it is relatively low-carb, it does not restrict carbohydrates to the same degree as the keto diet, and therefore does not engage ketosis. The keto diet, on the other hand, focuses primarily on the three macronutrients of fat, protein, and carbohydrates. By consuming a lot of fat but not very much protein and very few carbs, someone on the keto diet can induce ketosis, a metabolic state in which the body burns fat instead of carbohydrates for energy. The big, shiny difference between the two is ketosis—teaching your body to keep burning fat—and that is what we're after.

Benefits of Diary-Free Keto

People choose to go dairy-free for a number of reasons. Perhaps the most common is lactose intolerance (the inability to digest lactose, the sugar found in milk)—which 65 percent of people in the world have, according to the National Institutes of Health. There are a host of additional medical conditions and symptoms that can be negatively impacted by dairy consumption, and it's important to check in with your health and assess whether eliminating dairy might help you achieve your specific desires and goals. If you have any of the following conditions, consider whether dairy-free might be the right modifier for your keto diet. It certainly was for me.

Stomach Pain: When stomach pain results from food sensitivities, it can be difficult to pinpoint the problem. An elimination diet can be helpful, and often, the problem turns out to be dairy products. In my case, my stomach was often hurting and uneasy, even after I had adapted to the keto diet. Once I went dairy-free, the problem was solved.

Severe Bloating: The inability to break down lactose can lead to major digestive problems, including gas and bloating. For those already prone to inflammation, dairy can aggravate the symptoms.

Constipation: Many people prone to constipation are sensitive to certain ingredients, dairy being one of them.

Gut Health: The impact of dietary changes on the human microbiome (the trillions of bacteria, viruses, and fungi that make up much of the body) is a constantly expanding area of science. According to the T.H. Chan School of Public Health at Harvard University, certain dietary influences can cause a disturbance in the balance of coexisting microbiota in the body. It wasn't until dairy-free keto helped me heal my gut that I even realized this was the root of so many of my issues.

Lactose Intolerance: If you've been holding back from keto because you're lactose intolerant and it seems to involve so much butter and cheese, worry no more! You don't have to eat dairy to eat keto, and you can still reap all the benefits. It's also worth noting that many people are lactose intolerant and don't realize it; in fact, many of the symptoms listed on this page can often be traced back to an absence of lactase, the enzyme that breaks down lactose. If you have even mild issues with certain dairy products, it's something to consider.

Stalled Weight Loss: If you feel like you're doing everything right and still can't get past that stubborn weight-loss plateau, try eliminating dairy. It might just be exactly what your body needs—either because of the conditions named above, such as bloating and lactose intolerance, or simply because it will change your caloric intake.

Polycystic Ovary Syndrome (PCOS): According to the U.S. Department of Health and Human Services, PCOS is "one of the most common endocrine disorders among women of reproductive age." Although current studies are inconclusive, it's possible that PCOS symptoms can be aggravated by dairy intake. Further research is needed to draw firm conclusions, but the anecdotal evidence was enough to convince me it was worth a try—and now I can add my own story to that list.

Irritable Bowel Syndrome (IBS): Most people with IBS are lactose intolerant, so keeping your diet dairy-free will help alleviate IBS symptoms and aid with stomach comfort.

Diary-Free Keto Friendly Ingredients in Your Pantry

- Almond flour
- Alternative sweeteners, such as Swerve (granulated and confectioners')
- Baking powder
- Bone broth
- Cayenne Coconut flour
- Coconut milk, canned
- Coconut, shredded
- Grapeseed oil
- Olive oil Pepper, black
- Salt, such as Himalayan pink salt, which is loaded with minerals and trace nutrients; I use it on everything
- Vanilla extract, alcohol-free

Refrigerated Essentials

- Bacon Barbecue sauce, sugar-free, low-carb (such as Tessemae's brand)
- Broccoli
- Cauliflower
- Cream cheese, dairy-free (such as Kite Hill brand)
- Eggs
- Ketchup, sugar-free, low-carb (such as Primal Kitchen brand)
- Marinades, sugar-free, low-carb
- Mayonnaise, sugar-free, low-carb (such as Primal Kitchen brand)
- Meats, grass-fed
- Mustard, sugar-free, low-carb (such as Primal Kitchen brand)
- Pickles
- Plain yogurt, dairy-free (such as Kite Hill brand)
- Salami, sugar-free, low-carb
- Other vegetables and greens

Other Perishable Essentials

- Avocados
- Garlic
- Lemons
- Onions
- Tomatoes

The Deal with Ghee

Many people wonder if ghee, or clarified butter, is the exception to the dairy-free rule. I will not be using ghee throughout this book in order to keep it 100 percent dairy-free, but some people with lactose intolerance are able to tolerate ghee, as it has very low levels of lactose and is thus unlikely to cause a reaction. However, you should always know and understand your own tolerance levels and dietary preferences. For those who can and do use ghee, feel free to replace the oils in my recipes with equal amounts of ghee.

Cooking Equipment

To cook the recipe in this book. You don't necessarily need a bunch of fancy equipment in your kitchen. These are few key items you should have in your kitchen.

Cutting Board: Because you'll be cutting, dicing, and mincing fresh ingredients, you need a proper surface for safe and handy chopping.

Cast Iron Skillet: I love to cook with a cast iron skillet because it can go straight from stovetop to oven and is an excellent tool for searing and roasting meat. My cast iron skillet was my grandmother's, and every time I use it, I think of her (though I'm sure she wasn't cooking keto!).

Blender: Because we're creating dairy-free recipes, we lose many of the natural binders that help thicken and hold ingredients together. A blender will help quickly incorporate ingredients.

Good Knife: A good sharp knife is essential to make all of your ingredients come together (or apart!) more easily. I personally love Cutco-brand knives.

Baking Sheets: You can cook everything from salmon to cookies on a baking sheet, so it's great to have two or three 13-by-18-inch rimmed baking sheets on hand. Use nonstick pans or layer parchment paper for easy cleanup. Nice to Have Once you've started cooking more often, you might find you'd like a few extra tools to fill out your kitchen arsenal.

Stand Mixer: A stand mixer (rather than a handheld electric mixer) is really nice to have for baking. You can combine your ingredients at the same time as you chop, wash, or perform other kitchen tasks, thereby minimizing your prep time.

Baking Dishes: I use both 9-by-13-inch and 8-by-11-inch baking dishes a lot when I cook keto meals. Baking dishes have deeper sides than rimmed baking sheets, so they work for a wide range of recipes, from roasts to casseroles to desserts. Enameled cast iron baking sheets are pricey but conduct heat extremely well and are also versatile (they can even be used on the stovetop). Tempered glass (like Pyrex) or enameled ceramic baking dishes are the next best thing; they're durable and most are suitable for use with a wide range of oven temperatures.

Mixing Bowls: Having small, medium, and large mixing bowls makes cooking so much simpler. They're easy to store and wash, so you'll always have a clean one handy and appropriately sized for your ingredient (which helps avoid messes in the kitchen due to overfilled bowls).

Splatter Screen: A splatter screen is a game changer for stovetop cooking. You place the screen (usually made of stainless steel or silicone) on top of the active pan to catch any bubbling oils or splashes

Swap It Out!

NEED THIS	USE THIS INSTEAD
Butter for cooking	Olive oil, Avocado oil, Coconut oil
Butter for Spreading	Avocado, Coconut butter
Cream Cheese	Diary-free cream cheese
Greek Yogurt	Diary-free plain yogurt
Heavy Cream	Coconut cream (canned)
Cream for coffee	Diary-free creamers
Milk	Almond milk, cashew milk, coconut milk
Ranch dressing	Avocado oil-or sunflower oil-based dressings (I prefer Primal Kitchen or Tessemae's

Foods You Should Consume More

Meats

· Bison

· Beef

· Beef liver

· Pork

· Chicken

· Seafood

· Sausage (Without fillers)

· Turkey

Low-carb Veggies

· Avocados

· Asparagus

· Broccoli

· Brussels sprouts

· Cabbage

· Cauliflower

· Green beans

· Lettuce

· Kale

· Mushrooms

· Olives

· Okra

· Pickles

· Onions

· Radishes

· Scallions

· Shallots

· Spaghetti squash (in moderation)

Food You Should Consume in Moderation

Nuts & Seeds

· Almonds

· Chia seeds

· Cashews

· Flaxseeds

· Hazelnuts

· Macadamia nuts

· Nut butters

· Peanuts

· Pecans

· Pine nuts

· Pili nuts

· Pistachios

· Walnuts

· Pumpkin seeds

Berries

- Blueberries
- Blackberries
- Strawberries
- Raspberries

Artificial Sweeteners

- Erythritol (E.g. Swerve)
- Monk fruit sweetener
- Stevia

Foods to Avoid

Dairy

- Cream
- Cheese
- Cream Cheese
- Milk
- Yogurt

Carbs

- Breads
- Candy
- Pasta
- Corn
- Rice
- Potatoes
- Winter
- Squashes

Fruits

- Apricots
- Apples
- Bananas
- Dates

- Grapes
- Grapefruit
- Honeydew
- Kiwi
- Mangoes
- Oranges
- Peaches
- Prunes

Chapter Two: Breakfast & Brunch Recipes

Hot Chicken and Waffles (One Pot)

Serves: 6

Preparation time: 40 minutes

Ingredients

·   1 recipe Best Fried Chicken Ever

·   ¼ cup hot wing sauce

·   1 tablespoon cayenne

·   1 recipe Waffles

·   6 tablespoons sugar-free maple-flavored syrup (such as Choc Zero)

·   2 tablespoons Swerve confectioners

Directions

1.   In a bowl, toss the chicken in the hot sauce and cayenne.

2.   Arrange the chicken on top of the waffles, drizzle the syrup over the top, sprinkle with powdered sweetener, and serve immediately.

Nutritional Information: Calories: 572, Carbs: 22g, Fat: 48g, Fiber: 4g, Protein: 26g

Sausage Gravy

Serves: 8

Preparation time: 10 minutes

Cooking time: 20 minutes

Ingredients

· 2 tablespoons olive oil

· 1-pound pork sausage

· ½ white onion, diced

· 1 tablespoon minced garlic

· 1 (14-ounce) can coconut milk

· ¼ cup almond flour

· 1 teaspoon amaranth flour

· 1 teaspoon salt

· ½ teaspoon freshly ground pepper

Directions

1. Heat olive oil in a cast iron skillet over medium-high heat. Add sausage and cook, stirring and breaking up the meat with a spatula, until it begins to brown, about 2 minutes

2. Add the onions and garlic, then continue to cook. Stirring frequently, until the sausage is browned and the onion is soft, about 5 minutes.

3. Reduce the heat to medium and clear a space in the center of the meat mixture. Pour the coconut milk into the space. Then, stirring the milk constantly, add the almond and amaranth flours

4. Cook, stirring, until the milk and flours are well combined, about 5 minutes

5. Now stir the milk mixture and the meat together to mix well, and cook for another 3-5 minutes, or until thickened. Don't be alarmed if the texture is thinner than what you might be used to; it will still taste like an old-school, rich, creamy gravy

6. Season with the salt and pepper, and serve hot

Nutritional Information: Calories: 335, Carbs: 4g, Fat: 31g, Fiber: 1g, Protein:

10g

Iced Green Tea Latte

Serves: 8

Preparation time: 3 minutes

Ingredients

- ½ cup hot (not boiling) water
- 1 tablespoon matcha powder
- 8 ounces cold unsweetened cashew milk (or hemp milk if nut-free)
- 5 drops vanilla-flavored liquid stevia

Directions

1. Place the hot water and matcha powder in a blender and pulse until smooth.

2. Add the milk and sweetener and blend well. Pour into a glass over ice.

3. Serve fresh

Nutritional Information: Calories: 38, Carbs: 7g, Fat: 1g, Fiber: 1g, Protein: 1g

Cherry Almond Breakfast Shake

Serves: 2

Preparation time: 4 minutes

Ingredients

· 1 cup unsweetened cashew milk or almond milk (or coconut milk for a thicker drink)

· 1 cup strong brewed cherry or hibiscus tea, chilled (or more cashew milk)

· ¼ cup almond butter or Kite Hill brand cream cheese style spread

· 1 teaspoon cherry extract

· ½ teaspoon almond extract

· ¼ cup Swerve confectioners

· Pinch of fine sea salt Crushed ice

Directions

1. Place all of the ingredients, except the ice, in a blender and blend until smooth. Just before serving, add the crushed ice and puree again until smooth. Pour into 2 glasses and serve.

2. Store in an airtight container in the refrigerator.

Nutritional Information: Calories: 203, Carbs:7g, Fat: 18g, Fiber: 3g, Protein: 9g

Amazing Protein Shake

Serves: 4

Preparation time: 5 minutes

Ingredients

· 4 hard-boiled eggs (see here), peeled

· 1 (13½-ounce) can full-fat coconut milk

· 1 cup unsweetened almond milk (or hemp milk if nut-free)

· ½ cup Swerve confectioners'-style sweetener

· 1 teaspoon stevia glycerite, plus more to taste

· Seeds scraped from 2 vanilla beans (about 8 inches long), or 2 teaspoons vanilla extract ¼ cup unsweetened cocoa powder, plus more to taste

· 1 teaspoon ground cinnamon

· ⅛ teaspoon fine sea salt

Directions

1. Place all of the ingredients in a blender and puree until very smooth. Taste and add up to an additional teaspoon of stevia glycerite and more cocoa powder, if desired.

2. Store in an airtight container in the refrigerator for up to 4 days. The flavor of this shake is best after it sits for a day in the fridge.

Nutritional Information: Calories: 234, Carbs: 4g, Fat: 21g, Fiber: 2g, Protein: 8g

Baked Eggs and Ham

Serves: 4

Preparation time: 5 minutes

Ingredients

· 4 large eggs, beaten

· 4 slices ham, diced

· ½ teaspoon fine sea salt

· Pinch of ground black pepper

· Fresh herbs of choice, for garnish (optional)

Directions

1. Preheat the oven to 350°F. Grease two 4-ounce ramekins.

2. In a large bowl, whisk the eggs, ham, salt, and pepper until combined. Divide equally between the ramekins.

3. Place the ramekins in the oven and bake until the eggs are puffed and set in the center, 12 to 14 minutes. Garnish with fresh herbs, if desired.

4. Store in an airtight container in the refrigerator for up to 3 days. To reheat, place in a preheated 350°F oven for 5 minutes or until warmed through.

Nutritional Information: Calories: 285, Carbs: 7g, Fat: 19g, Fiber: 0.1g, Protein: 25g

French Toast Cereal

Serves: 1

Preparation time: 15 minutes

Ingredients

· 2 tablespoons melted coconut oil

· 2 tablespoons Swerve confectioners'-style sweetener or equivalent amount of liquid or powdered sweetener

· 1 teaspoon ground cinnamon

· ½ teaspoon maple or vanilla extract

· 1-ounce pork rinds, crumbled into

· ¼- to ½-inch pieces

· 1 cup unsweetened cashew milk or almond milk (or hemp milk if nut-free), for serving

Directions

1. Place the melted coconut oil, sweetener, cinnamon, and extract in a small bowl. Stir well to combine. Add the crumbled pork rinds and stir well to coat.

2. Cover and place the bowl in the refrigerator to chill for at least 10 minutes or until ready to eat (it will keep in an airtight container in the refrigerator for up to 3 days).

3. When ready to eat, uncover and break up the cereal a bit with a spoon. Just before serving, pour in the milk.

Nutritional Information: Calories: 426, Carbs: 4g, Fat: 42g, Fiber: 1g, Protein: 8g

Smoked Salmon, Egg, And Avocado

Serves: 1

Preparation time: 8 minutes

Ingredients

- 1 large egg
- 1 tablespoon distilled white vinegar
- 1 cup torn leafy lettuce
- 1 tablespoon Greek Vinaigrette or Cilantro Lime Dressing
- ¼ avocado, sliced
- 2 ounces smoked salmon
- Fine sea salt and ground black pepper

Directions

1. To poach the egg, bring a pot of water to a simmer. Add the vinegar, which will help the egg white hold together. Break the egg into a ramekin or small bowl. Rapidly swirl the water with a spoon.

2. Gently slide the egg into the simmering water and poach for about 3 minutes for just-set white and still-runny yolk (or cook the egg to your liking). Remove the poached egg with a slotted spoon and place on a paper towel to drain.

3. Place the lettuce on a plate and drizzle with the dressing. Top the lettuce with the sliced avocado, smoked salmon, and poached egg.

4. Season with salt and pepper to taste.

Sausage Breakfast Hash (One Pot)

Serves: 6

Preparation time: 15 minutes

Cooking time: 35 minutes

Ingredients

- 6 tablespoons olive oil
- 1-pound kielbasa, cut into ½-inch pieces
- 1 green bell pepper, seeded and chopped
- 1 red bell pepper, seeded and chopped
- 1 red onion, diced
- 1 jalapeño pepper, diced
- 3 garlic cloves, minced
- 1 teaspoon salt
- ½ teaspoon freshly ground black pepper
- 1 (14-ounce) can stewed tomatoes

Directions

1. In a large skillet, heat the oil over medium heat. Add the kielbasa and cook, stirring, until browned, about 5 minutes.

2. Add the green pepper, red pepper, onion, jalapeño, garlic, salt, and black pepper. Cook, stirring occasionally, for 10 to 12 minutes, until the vegetables are softened and browned.

3. Reduce the heat to medium-low, stir in the tomatoes, cover, and let simmer for 15 minutes. Serve hot.

Nutritional Information: Calories: 331, Carbs: 11g, Fat: 27g, Fiber: 2g, Protein: 11g

Radish Hash Browns with Onion and Green Pepper (One Pot)

Serves: 3

Preparation time: 5 minutes

Cooking time: 25 minutes

Ingredients

- 5 tablespoons olive oil
- 12 radishes, thinly sliced
- 1 onion, diced
- 1 green bell pepper, seeded and diced
- 6 garlic cloves, minced
- 1 teaspoon cayenne
- 1 teaspoon salt
- ½ teaspoon freshly ground black pepper

Directions

1. In a skillet over medium heat, heat the oil. Add the radishes, onion, bell pepper, and garlic. Cook, stirring frequently, until the vegetables are tender, about 5 minutes.

2. Add the cayenne, salt, and pepper. Continue to cook, stirring occasionally, for about 20 minutes, or until the vegetables are browned and crisp around the edges.

Nutritional Information: Calories: 252, Carbs: 8g, Fat: 24g, Fiber: 2g, Protein: 1g

Monte Cristo Sandwiches

Serves: 6

Preparation time: 10 minutes

Cooking time: 20 minutes

Ingredients

- 6 large eggs
- 1 teaspoon salt
- 1 teaspoon freshly ground black pepper
- 2 tablespoons olive oil
- 1 recipe Waffles
- 1 recipe Perfect Bacon
- ¼ cup low-carb syrup (like Choc Zero)
- 6 tablespoons Swerve confectioners' (or another powdered alternative sweetener)

Directions

1. In a small bowl, whisk together the eggs, salt, and pepper.

2. In a small skillet, heat the oil over medium heat. Add the egg mixture and cook, stirring continuously, until thoroughly cooked, about 6 minutes.

3. Top half of each waffle with some of the scrambled egg and 2 or 3 pieces of bacon. Fold the waffle over to make a sandwich and drizzle the syrup over the top. Sprinkle with the powdered sweetener and serve immediately.

Nutritional Information: Calories: 545, Carbs: 11g, Fat: 45g, Fiber: 2g, Protein: 29g

Rustic Egg Bites

Serves: 12

Preparation time: 20 minutes

Cooking time: 22 minutes

Ingredients

- 1 tablespoon avocado oil, plus more for greasing the muffin tin
- 1-pound ground sausage
- 12 large eggs
- ⅔ cup canned coconut milk
- 2 tablespoons minced garlic
- 1 tablespoon salsa
- 1 teaspoon salt
- ½ teaspoon freshly ground black pepper

Directions

1. Preheat the oven to 400°F. Grease a 12-cup muffin tin with oil.

2. In a large skillet over medium-high heat, cook the sausage, stirring and breaking up the meat with a spatula, until browned, about 5 minutes. Remove from the heat and let cool for a few minutes.

3. Crack the eggs into a medium mixing bowl and add the coconut milk, garlic, salsa, avocado oil, salt, and pepper. Whisk to combine.

4. Stir the cooked sausage into the egg mixture, then pour the mixture evenly into the prepared muffin tin. Bake in the preheated oven for 25 minutes.

5. Serve warm or store in an airtight container in the refrigerator for up to 1 week.

Nutritional Information: Calories: 243, Carbs: 3g, Fat: 19g, Fiber: 0g, Protein: 15g

Sun-Dried Tomato and Ham Omelet

Serves: 12

Preparation time: 5 minutes

Cooking time: 15-30 minutes

Ingredients

- 6 large eggs
- ½ cup canned coconut milk
- 1 teaspoon salt
- 1 teaspoon freshly ground black pepper
- ¼ cup coconut oil
- ½ cup fresh spinach
- ¾ cup diced ham
- 2 tablespoons sun-dried tomatoes

Directions

1. In a small bowl, whisk together the eggs, milk, salt, and pepper.

2. Heat the oil in a medium skillet over medium heat. Add the egg mixture and reduce the heat to medium-low.

3. Once the egg mixture begins to bubble on the sides, add the spinach, ham, and sun-dried tomatoes, and cook for 3 minutes.

4. Using a spatula, fold over the eggs once to make a half-moon shape.

5. Flip carefully and continue cooking for 3 to 5 additional minutes.

6. Transfer to a plate and serve.

Nutritional Information: Calories: 646, Carbs: 5g, Fat: 54g, Fiber: 3g, Protein: 30g

Crustless Quiche with Ham, Mushrooms, And Onion

Serves: 8

Preparation time: 20 minutes

Cooking time: 70 minutes

Ingredients

- 2 tablespoons olive oil, plus more for greasing the pie plate
- 10 large eggs
- 2 cups diced ham
- 1 cup mushrooms
- 1 white onion, diced
- ½ cup canned coconut milk
- 1 tablespoon garlic powder
- 1 teaspoon salt
- ½ teaspoon freshly ground black pepper
- 2 tablespoons minced fresh chives

Directions

1. Preheat the oven to 400°F.

2. Grease a 9-inch glass pie plate.

3. In a large mixing bowl, stir together the eggs, ham, mushrooms, onion, coconut milk, olive oil, garlic powder, salt, and pepper. Pour the mixture into the greased pie plate.

4. Bake for 1 hour 10 minutes, until the center is set and the top is golden brown.

5. Serve immediately, garnished with the chives, or wrap and store in the refrigerator for up to 1 week.

Nutritional Information: Calories: 220, Carbs: 5g, Fat: 16g, Fiber: 2g, Protein: 14g

Loaded Scrambled Eggs

Serves: 2

Preparation time: 4 minutes

Cooking time: 8 minutes

Ingredients

- 1 tablespoon butter-flavored coconut oil or bacon fat
- ¼ cup sliced mushrooms
- ¼ cup diced red bell peppers
- 2 tablespoons diced onions
- 4 large eggs, beaten
- ¼ teaspoon fine sea salt
- ⅛ teaspoon ground black pepper
- ¼ cup diced ham

For Garnish:

- Sliced scallions
- Fresh parsley leaves

Directions

1.   Heat the coconut oil in a skillet over medium heat. Add the mushrooms, peppers, and onions and sauté for 5 minutes or until the mushrooms turn golden.

2.   Meanwhile, whisk the eggs in a bowl with the salt, pepper, and 2 tablespoons of water. Add the ham and stir to combine.

3.   Pour the egg and ham mixture into the skillet with the mushroom mixture. Scramble over medium heat until the eggs are cooked to your liking. Serve garnished with sliced scallions and parsley.

4.   Store in an airtight container in the refrigerator for up to 3 days. To reheat, place the eggs in a greased skillet over medium heat for a few minutes, until warmed to your liking.

Nutritional Information: Calories: 281, Carbs: 2g, Fat: 22g, Fiber: 2g, Protein: 19g

Homestyle Fried Eggs (One Pot)

Serves: 2 Eggs

Preparation time: 2 minutes

Cooking time: 5 minutes

Ingredients

- 3 tablespoons olive oil or avocado oil
- 2 large eggs
- 1 teaspoon salt
- ½ teaspoon freshly ground black pepper

Directions

1. In a small skillet over high heat, heat the oil, tilting the pan to coat.

2. Crack the eggs into the hot oil. Season with the salt and pepper.

3. Remove from the heat, and let the eggs continue to cook for about 3 minutes, until the whites are set and the edges are browned and crisp. Serve hot.

Nutritional Information: Calories: 382, Carbs: 1g, Fat: 37g, Fiber: 0g, Protein: 13g

Breakfast Asparagus

Serves: 1

Preparation time: 4 minutes

Cooking time: 15 minutes

Ingredients

· 6 asparagus spears

· 2 strips bacon, diced

· 2 large eggs

· 1½ teaspoons chopped fresh chives

· ¼ teaspoon fine sea salt

· ⅛ teaspoon ground black pepper

Directions

1. Trim the woody ends off the asparagus.

2. Cook the bacon in a cast-iron skillet over medium heat until crispy, about 5 minutes. Remove the bacon from the skillet, leaving the drippings in the pan.

3. Add the asparagus to the hot pan and cook until crisp-tender, 5 to 6 minutes (depending on the thickness of the asparagus). Crack the eggs into the pan, over the asparagus. Sprinkle with the chives, salt, and pepper.

4. Lower the heat to medium-low and cook just until the egg whites are set and the yolks are still runny. Garnish with the reserved bacon.

Nutritional Information: Calories: 335, Carbs: 1g, Fat: 24g, Fiber: 2g, Protein: 25g

Perfect Bacon (One Pot)

Serves: 4

Preparation time: 5 minutes

Cooking time: 22 minutes

Ingredients

· 1 (12-ounce) package bacon (8 to 12 strips)

Direction

1. Preheat the oven to 400°F.

2. Line a large baking sheet with two pieces of parchment paper.

3. Arrange the bacon strips in a single layer on the prepared sheet.

4. Cook in the preheated oven for 22 minutes.

5. Let cool slightly before serving.

Nutritional Information: Calories: 100, Carbs: 0g, Fat: 8g, Fiber: 0g, Protein: 7g

Spicy Fried Eggs with Chorizo

Serves: 4

Preparation time: 4 minutes

Cooking time: 12 minutes

Ingredients

· 1 tablespoon lard or coconut oil

· ¼ cup diced red bell peppers

· 2 tablespoons diced onions

· 1 small jalapeño pepper, seeded and finely diced (optional)

· 4 ounces Mexican-style fresh (raw) chorizo, removed from casings

· 4 large eggs

· ¼ teaspoon fine sea salt

· ⅛ teaspoon ground black pepper

· Fresh cilantro leaves, for garnish

Directions

1. Heat the lard in a cast-iron skillet or nonstick pan over medium heat. Add the red bell peppers, onions, and jalapeño, if using. Sauté until the onions are soft, about 4 minutes. Add the chorizo and cook while crumbling for 3 minutes or until cooked through. Remove from the pan and set aside.

2. Add another teaspoon of coconut oil to the pan, if needed. Crack the eggs into the skillet. Season with the salt and pepper. Cover and cook until the whites are cooked and the yolks are done to your liking, about 4 minutes for still-runny yolks. Divide the eggs between 2 serving plates. Place the chorizo mixture over the eggs and enjoy!

3. Store in an airtight container in the refrigerator for up to 3 days. To reheat, place in a greased skillet over medium heat for a few minutes, until warmed to your liking.

Nutritional Information: Calories: 379, Carbs: 0g, Fat: 31g, Fiber: 1g, Protein: 19g

Lemon Poppyseed Waffles

Serves: 4

Preparation time: 4 minutes

Cooking time: 4 minutes

Ingredients

- 4 large eggs
- 4 hard-boiled eggs, peeled
- ¼ cup coconut oil
- ¼ cup Swerve confectioners'-style sweetener
- 2 tablespoons unflavored
- 2 tablespoons lemon juice
- 2 tablespoons poppy seeds
- 2 teaspoons lemon extract, or 6 drops lemon oil
- ¾ teaspoon baking powder
- ¼ teaspoon fine sea salt
- ¼ cup Lemon Syrup, for serving

Directions

1. Heat a waffle iron to high heat.

2. Place the raw eggs, hard-boiled eggs, coconut oil, sweetener, protein powder, lemon juice, poppy seeds, extract, baking powder, and salt in a blender or food processor and pulse until smooth and thick.

3. Grease the hot waffle iron. Place 3 tablespoons of the batter in the center of the iron and close. Cook for 3 to 4 minutes, until the waffle is golden brown and crisp. Repeat with the remaining batter, regreasing the waffle iron as needed. Serve with the syrup.

4. Store in an airtight container in the refrigerator for up to 3 days or in the freezer for up to a month. To reheat, place in a toaster oven or in a preheated 375°F oven for 3 minutes or until warmed to your liking.

Nutritional Information: Calories: 268, Carbs: 2g, Fat: 15, Fiber: 0.5g, Protein: 15g

Waffles

Serves: 6

Preparation time: 10 minutes

Cooking time: 20 minutes

Ingredients

- 1 (8-ounce) container of dairy-free cream cheese (such as Kite Hill)
- 7 large eggs
- 1½ tablespoons cinnamon
- 4 teaspoons Swerve granular
- 2 tablespoons olive oil, divided Sugar-free maple-flavored syrup, for serving

Directions

1. In a large microwave-safe bowl, heat the cream cheese in the microwave for 45 seconds. Use a wire whisk to whip until fluffy.

2. Add the eggs and continue to whip until the mixture is well combined and thick. Stir in the cinnamon, sweetener, and 1 tablespoon of oil.

3. Liberally grease the waffle iron with the remaining 1 tablespoon of oil and pour the batter in the iron ¼ cup at a time. Cook according to the waffle iron manufacturer's instructions.

4. Serve hot, topped with syrup.

Nutritional Information: Calories: 227, Carbs: 3g, Fat: 19g, Fiber: 0g, Protein: 9g

Breakfast Sausage Soup

Serves: 6

Preparation time: 15 minutes

Cooking time: 15 minutes

Ingredients

· 1 tablespoon avocado oil

· 1-pound bulk breakfast sausage

· ½ cup diced onions

· 2 large cloves garlic, minced

· 1 teaspoon minced fresh sage

· 3 cups chicken bone broth, homemade

· 1 cup tomato sauce ½ teaspoon fine sea salt

· ½ teaspoon ground black pepper

· 6 large eggs (omit for egg-free)

For Garnish (Optional)

· Diced avocado Fresh herbs, such as thyme

Directions

1. Heat the oil in a Dutch oven or stockpot over medium heat. Add the sausage, onions, garlic, and sage and cook for about 6 minutes, breaking up the sausage into small chunks as it browns.

2. Add ¼ cup of the chicken broth to the pot and scrape the bottom to deglaze.

3. Add the remaining chicken broth, tomato sauce, salt, and pepper and simmer over medium heat for 8 minutes. Taste and adjust the seasoning.

4. Meanwhile, make the soft-boiled eggs: Fill a medium-sized saucepan halfway with water and bring the water just to a simmer. Gently place the eggs in the simmering water one at a time. Cook the eggs for 5 to 6 minutes, depending on how runny you prefer the yolks: 5 minutes will give you runny yolks and 6 minutes will give you yolks that are just set. Make sure to hold the water at a simmer; don't let it come to a boil. Remove the eggs and run under cool water for 30 seconds. Once cool, carefully peel the eggs and slice them in half.

5.   Ladle the soup into bowls, then top each bowl with the eggs. Garnish with diced avocado and fresh herbs, if desired.

6.   Store in an airtight container in the refrigerator for up to 3 days. To reheat, place the soup in a saucepan over medium heat for 3 minutes or until warmed through.

Nutritional Information: Calories: 379, Carbs: 5g, Fat: 31g, Fiber: 1g, Protein:20g

Keto Faux Cappuccino (One Pot)

Serves: 1

Preparation time: 10 minutes

Ingredients

· ¼ cup nut milk

· 1 scoop vanilla-flavored collagen

· 1 scoop MCT oil powder

· 1 cup brewed coffee

Directions

1. Combine the nut milk, collagen, and MCT oil powder in an electric frothier or a coffee cup. Froth until fluffy and thick. (If using a handheld frothier, heat the mixture for about 20 seconds in the microwave beforehand.)

2. Combine the froth mixture with the coffee and enjoy immediately.

Nutritional Information: Calories: 183, Carbs: 6g, Fat: 11g, Fiber: 0g, Protein: 13g

Irish Breakfast

Serves: 4

Preparation time: 8 minutes

Cooking time: 15 minutes

Ingredients

·   4 strips bacon

·   4 breakfast sausage links (precooked)

·   2 tablespoons lard or bacon fat, or more if needed

·   1 cup sliced button mushrooms

·   Fine sea salt

·   4 large eggs

·   Ground black pepper

·   1 small tomato, quartered

·   1 Keto Brioche

·   Chopped fresh parsley or other herb of choice, for garnish

Directions

1.   Cook the bacon in a large cast-iron skillet over medium-high heat until crispy, about 5 minutes. Remove to a platter, leaving the fat in the skillet. Add the sausages and cook, turning occasionally, until browned, about 3 minutes. Remove from the skillet and set on the platter with the bacon, leaving the drippings in the pan.

2.   Add the lard to the skillet and heat until melted. Add the mushrooms and season with salt. Sauté until the mushrooms are golden, about 3 minutes. Remove the mushrooms and set on the platter with the meat.

3.   Crack the eggs into the skillet. Season with salt and pepper. Cover and cook until the whites are set and the yolks are cooked to your liking. Remove to the platter with the meat and mushrooms.

4.   If the skillet is dry, add a little more lard. Add the tomato quarters to the hot skillet and season with salt and pepper. Slice the brioche into ¼-inch-thick slices and place in the skillet with the tomatoes. Fry the tomatoes and brioche for 2

minutes per side. Remove from the skillet and place on the platter. Garnish with fresh herbs and serve.

Nutritional Information: Calories: 305, Carbs: 2g, Fat: 26g, Fiber: 1g, Protein: 16g

Cauliflower Oatmeal with Blueberries

Serves: 2

Preparation time: 5 minutes

Cooking Time: 15 minutes

Ingredients

- 1 (12-ounce) bag riced cauliflower
- 1 (14-ounce) can coconut milk
- 2 tablespoons walnut oil
- 2 tablespoons peanut butter powder
- 2 tablespoons sugar-free maple syrup (such as Choc Zero)
- 10 blueberries

Direction

1. In a medium saucepan, combine the cauliflower and coconut milk and bring to a boil over medium-high heat.

2. Reduce the heat to medium-low and stir in the walnut oil, peanut butter powder, and syrup. Cook, stirring occasionally, for 10 minutes.

3. Serve immediately, topped with the blueberries.

Nutritional Information: Calories: 684, Carbs: 27g, Fat: 60g, Fiber: 0g, Protein: 9g

Reuben Eggs Benedict

Serves: 2

Preparation time: 6 minutes

Cooking Time: 5 minutes

Ingredients

· 1 Keto Brioche

· 1½ teaspoons coconut oil or lard, for frying

· 4 large eggs

· 8 slices corned beef

· ¼ cup fermented sauerkraut

Thousand Island Dressing

· 3 tablespoons mayonnaise, homemade or store-bought

· 1 tablespoon chopped dill pickles

· 1 tablespoon tomato sauce

· Pinch of fine sea salt

Directions

1. Cut the brioche into four ½-inch-thick slices. Fry in a skillet with the coconut oil until golden brown and toasted.

2. Meanwhile, poach the eggs following the method described on here.

3. While the eggs are poaching, prepare the dressing: Place the mayo, pickles, tomato sauce, and salt in a small dish and stir well to combine.

4. Place 2 slices of corned beef on each brioche slice. Top each with 1 tablespoon sauerkraut, a poached egg, and 1 tablespoon of dressing.

5. Store in an airtight container in the refrigerator for up to 3 days. To reheat, place on a rimmed baking sheet in a 400°F oven for 4 minutes or until warmed through.

Nutritional Informational: Calories: 546, Carbs: 2g, Fat: 60g, Fiber: 0.1g, Protein: 45g

Silky Egg Breakfast Soup

Serves: 2

Preparation time: 5 minutes

Cooking Time: 5 minutes

Ingredients

· 2 cups chicken bone broth, homemade or store-bought

· 5 large eggs, beaten

· 2½ tablespoons fish sauce

· 2 cups diced leftover cooked chicken

· Fine sea salt (optional)

· Juice of 1 lime

For Garnish

· Fresh cilantro leaves

· Sliced scallions (sliced on the bias)

· Lime wedges

· Freshly ground black pepper

Directions

1.   Bring the broth to a boil in a large pot over medium-high heat. Slowly add the beaten eggs while whisking the broth. Reduce the heat to low and cook for 2 more minutes. Add the fish sauce and leftover chicken and continue cooking until the chicken is heated through. Taste and add salt, if needed. Add the lime juice and stir well.

2.   Pour the soup into bowls and garnish with cilantro, scallions, lime wedges, and freshly ground pepper.

3.   Store in an airtight container in the refrigerator for up to 3 days. Reheat the soup in a pot over medium heat for 5 minutes or until warmed through.

Nutritional Information: Calories: 521, Carbs: 5g, Fat: 60g, Fiber: 1g, Protein: 9g

Breakfast Sandwich

Serves: 2

Preparation time: 4 minutes

Cooking Time: 4 minutes

Ingredients

- 1 teaspoon coconut oil, avocado oil, or bacon fat
- 2 large eggs
- ¼ teaspoon fine sea salt
- ⅛ teaspoon ground black pepper
- 2 ounces shaved ham
- 1 slice tomato
- ¼ avocado, sliced
- 1 slice red onion

Directions

1. Heat the oil in a cast-iron skillet over medium heat.

2. Place 2 mason jar rings face down in the skillet. Crack an egg into each ring to form a perfect circle for the "bun" of your sandwich. Season the eggs with the salt and pepper. Use a fork to scramble the eggs a little and break up the yolks. Cover and cook until the eggs are cooked through, about 4 minutes.

3. Meanwhile, place the ham in the skillet to warm through.

4. Remove the eggs from the skillet. Place an egg on a plate. Top with the tomato slice, warm ham, and slices of avocado and red onion. Top with the other egg "bun."

Nutritional Information: Calories: 455, Carbs: 5g, Fats: 35g, Fiber: 3g, Protein 31g

Chapter Three: Staples, Sauces & Dressings

Red Pepper Dry Rub (One Pot)

Serves: ¼ cup

Preparation time: 10 minutes

Ingredients

- 2 teaspoons red pepper flakes
- 2 teaspoons salt
- 1½ teaspoons granulated garlic
- 1½ teaspoons onion powder
- 1½ teaspoons freshly ground black pepper
- 1 teaspoon dry mustard
- 1 teaspoon ground cumin
- ½ teaspoon cloves
- ½ teaspoon dried sage

Directions

1. In a small bowl or jar, combine the red pepper flakes, salt, granulated garlic, onion powder, pepper, dry mustard, cumin, cloves, and sage. Use immediately or store in an airtight container.

Nutritional Information: Calories: 6, Carbs: 1g, Fat: 0g, Fiber: 0g, Protein: 0g

Everything Marinade (One Pot)

Serves: ½ cup

Preparation time: 10 minutes

Ingredients

- 6 tablespoons olive oil
- 3 tablespoons white vinegar
- 1 teaspoon red pepper flakes
- 1 teaspoon whole-grain mustard
- 1 teaspoon salt
- 1 teaspoon freshly ground black pepper
- 1 teaspoon minced garlic

Directions

1. In a small bowl or large zip-top bag, mix the oil, vinegar, red pepper flakes, mustard, salt, pepper, and garlic. Use immediately or store in an airtight container for up to 2 weeks.

Nutritional Information: Calories: 93, Carbs: 1g, Fat: 11g, Fiber: 0g, Protein: 0g

Lemon-Garlic Dressing

Serves: ½ cup

Preparation time: 10 minutes

Ingredients

·   Zest and juice of 1 large lemon

·   6 garlic cloves, minced

·   1 teaspoon salt

·   1 teaspoon freshly ground black pepper

·   ½ teaspoon Swerve granular (or another granulated alternative sweetener)

·   ¾ cup olive oil

Directions

1.   In a small bowl, whisk together the lemon zest and juice, garlic, salt, pepper, and sweetener.

2.   While whisking, add the olive oil in a thin stream and whisk until the mixture emulsifies. Use immediately or store in an airtight container in the refrigerator for up to 2 weeks.

Nutritional Information: Calories: 223, Carbs: 2g, Fat: 25g, Fiber: 0g, Protein: 0g

Pico De Gallo (One Pot)

Serves: 2 cups

Preparation time: 15 minutes

Ingredients

- 1 large jalapeño pepper, diced
- ½ red onion, diced
- 10 cherry tomatoes, diced
- 8 garlic cloves, minced
- 3 tablespoons avocado oil
- 1½ teaspoons salt
- ½ teaspoon freshly ground black pepper

Directions

1. In a small bowl, combine the jalapeño, onion, tomatoes, and garlic.

2. Add the avocado oil, salt, and black pepper, and mix to combine. Serve immediately or store in an airtight container in the refrigerator for up to 5 days.

Nutritional Information: Calories: 61, Carbs: 3g, Fat: 5g, Fiber: 0g, Protein: 1g

Guacamole

Serves: 2 ½ cups

Preparation time: 20 minutes

Ingredients

- 3 avocados, halved, pitted, and peeled
- ½ red onion, diced
- 1 small tomato, diced
- 1 jalapeño pepper, diced (optional)
- 1 teaspoon garlic salt
- ½ teaspoon freshly ground black pepper

Directions

1. In a small bowl, mash the avocados with a fork until desired consistency is achieved. (I prefer my guacamole chunky.)

2. Add the onion, tomato, and jalapeño (if using), and stir to combine. 3Add the garlic salt and black pepper. Stir and serve immediately.

Nutritional Information: Calories: 200, Carbs: 11g, Fat: 16g, Fiber: 8g, Protein: 3g

Tartar Sauce (One Pot)

Serves: 1 cup

Preparation time: 5 minutes

Ingredients

· 1 cup sugar-free mayonnaise (like Primal Kitchen)

· 3 tablespoons chopped dill pickles

· 1 teaspoon yellow mustard

· 1 teaspoon Swerve granular

Directions

1. In a small bowl or jar, whisk or shake together the mayonnaise, pickles, mustard, and sweetener.

2. Use immediately or store in an airtight container in the refrigerator for up to 1 week.

Nutritional Information: Calories: 211, Carbs: 1g, Fat: 23g, Fiber: 0g, Protein: 0g

Pickled Cucumbers and Onions

Serves: 6

Preparation time: 10 minutes

Ingredients

- 5 or 6 baby cucumbers, diced
- 1 large white onion, diced
- 1 cup white vinegar
- 2 teaspoons chopped fresh dill
- 1½ teaspoons salt
- 1 teaspoon freshly ground black pepper
- 1 teaspoon olive oil

Directions

1. In a mason jar or other airtight container, combine the cucumbers, onion, vinegar, dill, salt, pepper, and olive oil. Serve immediately or cover and store in the refrigerator for up to 2 weeks.

Nutritional Information: Calories: 62, Carbs: 10g, Fat: 2g, Fiber: 2g, Protein: 2g

Cream Cheese Icing (One Pot)

Serves: 1 ½ cups

Preparation time: 10 minutes

Ingredients

·   1 (8-ounce) container dairy-free cream cheese (such as Kite Hill), at room temperature

·   ¼ cup Swerve confectioners' (or another powdered alternative sweetener)

·   1 teaspoon vanilla extract

Directions

1.   In a small bowl, blend together the cream cheese, sweetener, and vanilla. Use immediately or refrigerate to stiffen.

2.   Store covered in the refrigerator for up to 1 week.

Nutritional Information: Calories: 68, Carbs: 3g, Fat: 4g, Fiber: 0g, Protein: 3g

Chocolate Sauce

Serves: 1 cup

Preparation time: 10 minutes

Cooking time: 15 minutes

Ingredients

·   1 cup cacao butter

·   1 heaping tablespoon raw cacao powder (see tip)

·   2 tablespoons Swerve confectioners' (or another powdered alternative sweetener)

Directions

1.   In a small saucepan, melt the cacao butter over medium-low heat.

2.   While stirring continuously, add the cacao powder and sweetener. Cook, stirring, until the sweetener is dissolved, about 15 minutes.

3.   Serve hot for dipping, store in an airtight container in the refrigerator for up to 2 weeks or freeze for up to 3 months.

Nutritional Information: Calories: 133, Carbs: 0.5g, Fat: 14g, Fiber: 0g, Protein: 1g

Chapter Four: Small Bites and Drinks

Virgin Strawberry Margarita

Serves: 4

Preparation time: 4 minutes

Ingredients

·   Medium-coarse sea salt

·   Lime wedge

·   2 cups strong brewed hibiscus tea, chilled

·   ¼ cup Swerve confectioners'-style sweetener

·   ¼ cup lime juice

·   2 teaspoons strawberry extract

·   Ice, for serving

·   4 lime wedges, for garnish

Directions

1.   To coat the rims of the glasses, if desired, fill a saucer with about 1/8 inch of medium-coarse sea salt. Run a lime wedge around the rims of 4 tumblers. Take one of the glasses and roll the edge of the dampened rim in the salt until the entire rim is coated. Repeat with the other 3 glasses.

2.   Place the tea, sweetener, lime juice, and extract in a blender and blend until smooth. To serve, carefully fill the salt-rimmed tumblers with ice. Pour the margarita mixture into the glasses and garnish with lime wedges.

3.   Store in a pitcher in the refrigerator for up to 5 days. Stir well before serving.

Nutritional Information: Calories: 4, Carbs: 1g, Fat: 0g, Fiber: 0.1g, Protein: 0g

Devilish Deviled Eggs

Serves: 12

Preparation time: 15 minutes

Ingredients

- 12 hard-boiled eggs (see here), peeled and halved
- ½ cup mashed avocado
- 1 tablespoon Baconnaise (here) or mayonnaise
- 1 teaspoon lime juice
- ½ teaspoon fine sea salt
- ½ teaspoon onion powder
- 1 large baby red bell pepper, cut into 48 small triangles

Directions

1. Remove the egg yolks and place them in a bowl (or a food processor). Mash the yolks with a fork (or pulse in the food processor) until they have the texture of very fine crumbles.

2. Add the mashed avocado, Baconnaise, lime juice, salt, and onion powder to the egg yolks and mix until smooth. Fill the egg white halves with the yolk mixture.

3. Garnish with the red bell pepper triangles for "horns."

4. Store leftovers in an airtight container in the refrigerator for up to 3 days.

Nutritional Information: Calories: 83, Carbs: 1g, Fat: 7g, Fiber: 0.1g, Protein: 0g

Moroccan Deviled Eggs

Serves: 12

Preparation time: 6 minutes

Ingredients

·   12 hard-boiled eggs, peeled and halved

·   ¼ cup mayonnaise

·   3 tablespoons harissa paste

·   ½ teaspoon fine sea salt

For Garnish

·   Chopped fresh chives

·   Chopped fresh cilantro

Directions

1.   Remove the egg yolks and place them in a bowl (or a food processor). Mash the yolks with a fork (or pulse in the food processor) until they have the texture of very fine crumbles. Add the mayonnaise, harissa paste, and salt and mix until smooth.

2.   Fill the egg whites with the egg yolk mixture. Garnish with the chives and cilantro.

3.   Store in an airtight container in the refrigerator for up to 4 days.

Nutritional Information: Calories: 90, Carbs: 1g, Fat: 8g, Fiber: 0g, Protein: 6g

Shrimp Cocktail

Serves: 8

Preparation time: 5 minutes

Ingredients

- ¾ cup tomato sauce
- 1 tablespoon prepared horseradish, or more to taste
- 1 tablespoon lemon juice
- 1 to 2 teaspoons Swerve confectioners'-style sweetener
- ½ teaspoon onion powder
- ½ teaspoon fine sea salt
- 1-pound precooked large shrimp
- 1 lemon, sliced into wedges, for serving (optional)

Directions

1. Make the sauce: Place the sauce ingredients in a small bowl and stir well to combine. Adjust the seasoning to taste.

2. Serve the shrimp with the cocktail sauce, with lemon wedges on the side, if desired. 3.

3. Store in an airtight container in the refrigerator for up to 3 days.

Nutritional Information: Calories: 76, Carbs: 2g, Fat: 1g, Fiber: 14g, Protein: 14g

Pico De Gallo

Serves: 2 ½ cups

Preparation time: 7 minutes

Ingredients

· 1 large tomato, diced (about 1½ cups)

· ½ cup chopped white onions (about 1 medium)

· 2 cloves garlic, minced

· 2 tablespoons lime juice

· 2 tablespoons chopped fresh cilantro

· 1 jalapeño pepper, seeded and finely diced

· ½ teaspoon fine sea salt

Directions

1. Place all of the ingredients in a small bowl and stir until well combined.

2. Store in an airtight container in the refrigerator for up to 5 days.

Nutritional Information: Calories: 32, Carbs: 2g, Fat: 0.1g, Fiber: 1g, Protein: 1g

Citrus Avocado Salsa

Serves: 4

Preparation time: 5 minutes

Ingredients

- 1 cup diced tomatoes
- 1 small avocado, pitted and diced
- ¼ cup chopped fresh cilantro leaves
- 2 tablespoons avocado oil
- 4 drops orange oil, or 1 teaspoon orange extract
- Juice of 1 lime
- Fine sea salt and ground black pepper

Directions

1. Place the tomatoes, avocado, and cilantro in a small bowl. Add the avocado oil, orange oil, and lime juice and stir. Season to taste with salt and pepper.

2. Store in an airtight container in the refrigerator for up to 4 days.

Nutritional Information: Calories: 140, Carbs: 7g, Fat: 13g, Fiber: 3g, Protein: 1g

Virgin Strawberry Margarita

Serves: 4

Preparation time: 4 minutes

Ingredients

· Medium-coarse sea salt

· Lime wedge

· 2 cups strong brewed hibiscus tea, chilled

· ¼ cup Swerve confectioners'-style sweetener or equivalent amount of liquid or powdered sweetener

· ¼ cup lime juice

· 2 teaspoons strawberry extract Ice, for serving

· 4 lime wedges, for garnish

Directions

1. To coat the rims of the glasses, if desired, fill a saucer with about 1/8 inch of medium-coarse sea salt. Run a lime wedge around the rims of 4 tumblers. Take one of the glasses and roll the edge of the dampened rim in the salt until the entire rim is coated. Repeat with the other 3 glasses.

2. Place the tea, sweetener, lime juice, and extract in a blender and blend until smooth. To serve, carefully fill the salt-rimmed tumblers with ice. Pour the margarita mixture into the glasses and garnish with lime wedges.

3. Store in a pitcher in the refrigerator for up to 5 days. Stir well before serving.

Nutritional Information: Calories: 4, Carbs: 1g, Fat: 13g, Fiber: 0.1g, Protein: 0g

Chapter Four: Sea Foods

Fried Oysters in The Oven

Serves: 4

Preparation time: 20 minutes

Ingredients

- 3 tablespoons olive oil
- 1 teaspoon garlic salt
- 1 teaspoon freshly ground black pepper
- 1 teaspoon red pepper flakes
- 2 cups finely crushed pork rinds
- 24 shucked oysters

Directions

1. Preheat the oven to 400°F.

2. In a small bowl, mix together the olive oil, garlic salt, black pepper, and red pepper flakes.

3. Put the crushed pork rinds in a separate bowl.

4. Dip each oyster first in the oil mixture to coat and then in the pork rinds, turning to coat. Arrange the coated oysters on a baking sheet in a single layer with room in between.

5. Bake in the preheated oven for 30 minutes, or until the pork rind "breading" is browned and crisp. Serve hot.

Nutritional Information: Calories: 230, Carbs: 5g, Fat: 17g, Fiber: 0g, Protein: 15g

Tuna with Greens and Blueberries (One Pot)

Serves: 2

Preparation time: 10 minutes

Cooking time: 5 minutes

Ingredients

- ¼ cup olive
- 2 (4-ounce) tuna steaks
- Salt
- Freshly ground black pepper
- Juice of 1 lemon
- 4 cups salad greens
- ¼ cup low-carb, diary-free ranch dressing (Tessemae's)
- 2o blueberries

Directions

1. In a large skillet, heat the olive oil over medium-high heat.

2. Season the tuna steaks generously with salt and pepper, and add them to the skillet. Cook for 2 or 2 ½ minutes in each side to sear the outer edges.

3. Squeeze the lemon over the tuna in the pan and remove the fish

4. To serve, arrange the greens on 2 serving plates. Top each plate with one of the tuna steaks, 2 tablespoons of the ranch dressing, and 10 of the blueberries.

Nutritional Information: Calories: 549, Carbs: 7g, Fat: 41g, Fiber: 3g, Protein: 38g

Coconut Shrimp

Serves: 4

Preparation time: 20 minutes

Cooking time: 30 minutes

Ingredients

- Avocado oil spray (or other cooking oil spray)
- 3 large egg whites
- 1 teaspoon cayenne
- 1 teaspoon garlic salt
- 1 teaspoon freshly ground black pepper
- ½ teaspoon Swerve granular (or another granulated alternative sweetener)
- 1 cup unsweetened shredded coconut
- 24 (or so) raw shrimp, peeled

Directions

1. Preheat the oven to 350°F. Spray a large baking sheet with the avocado oil spray.

2. In a small bowl, whisk together the egg whites, cayenne, garlic salt, pepper, and sweetener.

3. Put the shredded coconut in a separate bowl.

4. One at a time, dunk the shrimp first in the egg mixture and then in the coconut, turning to coat completely.

5. Arrange the coated shrimp on the prepared baking sheet in a single layer, with room in between. Once all the shrimp have been coated, spray them lightly with avocado oil spray.

6. Bake in the preheated oven for 30 minutes, or until the coconut is golden brown.

Nutritional Information: Calories: 223, Carbs: 7g, Fat: 17g, Fiber: 4g, Protein: 13g

Bacon-Wrapped Scallop Cups (One Pot)

Serves: 4

Preparation time: 10 minutes

Cooking time: 25 minutes

Ingredients

- 12 large sea scallops
- 6 strips bacon, halved to make 12 short strips
- 24 garlic cloves, peeled but left whole
- 5 tablespoons Lemon-Garlic Dressing

Directions

1. Preheat the oven to 400°F.

2. Wrap each scallop with 1 piece of bacon. Use a toothpick to secure the bacon to the scallop. Arrange the wrapped scallops on a baking sheet.

3. Place 2 garlic cloves on top of each scallop, then top with a spoonful of the dressing. 4Bake for 25 minutes, or until the bacon is browned and crisp.

Nutritional Information: Calories: 374, Carbs: 9g, Fat: 26g, Fiber: 4g, Protein: 26g

Salmon Patties

Serves: 5

Preparation time: 10 minutes

Cooking time: 15 minutes

Ingredients

- 2 (6-ounce) cans boneless salmon
- 1 large egg
- 1½ tablespoons chopped fresh dill
- 1 teaspoon salt
- 1 teaspoon freshly ground black pepper
- 3 tablespoons olive oil

Directions

1. Mix together the salmon, egg, dill, salt and pepper in a small mixing bowl. Form the salmon mixture into hamburger-size patties

2. In a skillet over medium heat, heat the olive oil. Add the salmon patties to the skillet and cook for 3 to 4 minutes per side, or until golden brown and crisp. Serve hot

Nutritional Information: Calories: 198, Carbs: 1g, Fat: 14g, Fiber: 0g, Protein: 17g

Country Club Crab Cakes

Serves: 4

Preparation time: 10 minutes

Cooking time: 20 minutes

Ingredients

- 2 (6-ounce) cans crabmeat (or 12 ounces cooked crabmeat)
- 2 large eggs
- 2 tablespoons chopped fresh dill
- 1 teaspoon garlic salt
- ¼ cup olive oil

Directions

1. In a medium bowl, combine the crabmeat, eggs, dill, and garlic salt. Form the mixture into four patties.

2. In a medium skillet, heat the olive oil over medium heat. Cook the crab cakes for 3 to 4 minutes on each side, or until golden brown.

Nutritional Information: Calories: 212, Carbs: 1g, Fat: 16g, Fiber: 0g, Protein: 16g

Shrimp Sti-fry

Serves: 4

Preparation time: 10 minutes

Cooking time: 20 minutes

Ingredients

- ¼ cup avocado oil
- ¼ cup coconut aminos
- 2 cups chopped broccoli
- 1 onion, diced
- 1 red bell pepper, chopped
- 24 cooked and peeled shrimp
- 1 (12-ounce) bag riced cauliflower
- Chili sauce, for serving (Optional)

Directions

1.   Combine the shrimp, Cauliflower, onion, pepper, broccoli, coconut aminos, and avocado oil in a large skillet. Cook, stirring occasionally, until all the flavors are combined, about 20 minutes

2.   Drizzle the chili sauce over the top and serve hot

Nutritional Information: Calories: 231, Carbs: 12g, Fat: 15g, Fiber: 5g, Protein: 12g

Baked Salmon with Lemon and Mush

Serves: 2

Preparation time: 10 minutes

Cooking time: 30 minutes

Ingredients

· 2 (6-ounce) skin-on salmon fillets

· 1 onion, diced

· 8 ounces mushrooms, sliced

· ¼ cup olive oil

· 1 teaspoon salt

· 1 teaspoon freshly ground black pepper

· 4 lemon slices

Directions

1. Preheat the oven to 400°F.

2. Tear off 2 large squares of aluminum foil. Place a salmon fillet on each piece of foil and arrange the onion and mushrooms over and around the fish, dividing evenly.

3. Pour the olive oil over the fish, then season with the salt and pepper. Top each piece of fish with 2 lemon slices.

4. Wrap the foil up around the salmon and vegetables, leaving room inside the packet for heat to circulate, and bake for 30 minutes, or until the fish flakes easily with a fork. Serve hot.

Nutritional Information: Calories: 576, Carbs: 8g, Fat: 44g, Fiber: 3g, Protein: 37g

Pan-fried Soft Shell Crab

Serves: 2

Preparation time: 5 minutes

Cooking time: 10 minutes

Ingredients

- ½ cup olive oil
- ½ cup almond flour
- 1 teaspoon paprika
- 1 teaspoon garlic salt
- 1 teaspoon freshly ground black pepper
- 2 soft-shell crabs

Directions

1. Fill the bottom of a heavy skillet with the oil and heat over low heat.

2. While the oil is heating, in a medium bowl, mix together the almond flour, paprika, garlic salt, and pepper.

3. Dredge each crab in the flour mixture, coating both sides and shaking off any excess. Put the crabs into the hot oil in the skillet and cook for about 5 minutes per side, or until golden brown.

4. Serve hot.

Nutritional Information: Calories: 489, Carbs: 6g, Fat: 33g, Fiber: 2g, Protein: 42g

Mussels with Lemon-Garlic Sauce and Parsley (One Pot)

Serves: 5

Preparation time: 10 minutes

Cooking time: 5 minutes

Ingredients

· 36 live mussels, scrubbed and debearded

· 1 tablespoon olive oil

· 6 tablespoons Lemon-Garlic Dressing

· 2 tablespoons chopped fresh parsley, for garnish

Directions

1. Fill a stockpot halfway with water and bring it to a boil.

2. Add the mussels and olive oil to the boiling water and continue to boil for 4 minutes. Carefully drain off the water.

3. Pour the dressing over the mussels and serve immediately, garnished with the parsley.

Nutritional Information: Calories: 230, Carbs: 3g, Fat: 18g, Fiber: 1g, Protein: 14g

Three-Minute Lobster Tail

Serves: 2

Preparation time: 5 minutes

Cooking time: 5 minutes

Ingredients

- 4 cups bone broth (or water)
- 2 lobster tails

Directions

1. In a large pot, bring the broth to a boil.

2. While the broth is coming to a boil, use kitchen shears to cut the back side of the lobster shell from end to end.

3. Place the lobster in the boiling broth and bring it back to a boil. Cook the lobster for 3 minutes.

4. Drain and serve immediately.

Nutritional Information: Calories: 154, Carbs: 0g, Fat: 2g, Fiber: 0g, Protein: 32g

Chapter Five: Soups and Salads

Cauliflower and Bacon Soup

Serves: 8

Preparation time: 10 minutes

Cooking time: 1 hour

Ingredients

- 1 head cauliflower, stemmed and cut into large pieces
- 2 (14-ounce) cans coconut milk
- 2 cups bone broth
- 6 tablespoons olive oil, divided
- 1 onion, diced
- 1 cup sliced mushrooms
- 6 garlic cloves, minced
- 1½ teaspoons salt
- 1½ teaspoons freshly ground black pepper
- 1½ teaspoons cayenne
- 1 batch Perfect Bacon, chopped or crumbled

Directions

1. Fill a stockpot halfway with water and add the cauliflower. Bring to a boil and cook until the cauliflower is tender, about 20 minutes. Drain the cauliflower and then return it to the stockpot. Using a potato masher, mash the cauliflower until mostly smooth.

2. Put the pot over low heat and add the coconut milk and broth.

3. In a separate skillet, heat 3 tablespoons of oil over medium heat. Add the onion, mushrooms, and garlic. Cook, stirring frequently, for 15 to 20 minutes, or until softened.

4. Add the onion mixture to the soup mixture and continue cooking over low heat for 5 to 7 more minutes.

5.   Stir in the salt, pepper, cayenne, the remaining 3 tablespoons of oil, and the bacon. Cook for 20 minutes more.

6.   Serve immediately or store the soup in an airtight container in the refrigerator for up to 1 week.

Nutritional Information: Calories: 414, Carbs: 8g, Fat: 34g, Fiber: 4g, Protein: 19g

Hearty Vegetable Soup (One pot)

Serves: 8

Preparation time: 30 minutes

Cooking time: 8 hours

Ingredients

- 8 cups vegetable broth
- 2 (14-ounce) cans diced tomatoes
- 1 (16-ounce) bag kale, chopped
- 1 bunch radishes (about 12), halved
- 1 onion, chopped
- 2 celery stalks, chopped
- 2 cups fresh or frozen green beans, cut into 2-inch pieces
- 1 cup whole mushrooms
- 4 garlic cloves, minced
- ¼ cup olive oil

Directions

1. In a slow cooker, combine the vegetable broth, tomatoes, kale, radishes, onion, celery, green beans, mushrooms, garlic, and olive oil

2. Cover and cook on low for 8 hours. Serve hot

Nutritional Information: Calories: 168, Carbs: 15g, Fat: 8g, Fiber: 4g, Protein: 9g

Pizza Soup

Serves: 4

Preparation time: 6 minutes

Cooking time: 30 minutes

Ingredients

- 1 tablespoon avocado oil, coconut oil, or lard
- 2 cups sliced mushrooms
- ¼ cup diced onions
- ¼ cup diced red bell peppers
- 2 cloves garlic, minced
- 4 ounces Italian sausage, cut into ¼-inch pieces
- 4 ounces uncured pepperoni, cut into quarters
- 1 (25-ounce) jar pizza sauce or marinara sauce
- 1 (14½-ounce) can fire-roasted tomatoes
- 1 (3-ounce) can sliced black olives
- 1 tablespoon dried ground oregano
- ½ teaspoon fine sea salt
- Fresh oregano or basil leaves, for garnish

Directions

1. Heat the oil in a deep cast-iron skillet or pot over medium heat. Add the mushrooms and onions and sauté until the mushrooms are golden brown and the onions are soft, about 5 minutes. Add the bell peppers and garlic and sauté for another 2 minutes.

2. Add the sausage and sauté until cooked through, about 3 minutes. Add the pepperoni, pizza sauce, tomatoes, olives (if using), oregano, and salt. Cook for another 15 minutes. Taste and adjust the seasoning to your liking.

3. Ladle the soup into bowls. Garnish with oregano or basil leaves and serve.

4.   Store in an airtight container in the refrigerator for up to 3 days. To reheat, place the soup in a saucepan over medium heat for a few minutes, until warmed through.

Nutritional Information: Calories: 430, Carbs: 17g, Fat: 35g, Fiber: 5g, Protein: 15g

Cilantro Lime Meatball Soup

Serves: 8

Preparation time: 10 minutes

Cooking time: 35 minutes

Ingredients

- 2 pounds ground beef
- 1 cup finely chopped mushrooms
- ¼ cup chopped onions
- 2 cloves garlic, minced
- 1 pickled jalapeño pepper, seeded and finely chopped
- 1 teaspoon fine sea salt
- ½ teaspoon ground cumin
- 1 large egg
- 1 tablespoon lard or coconut oil
- ¼ cup chopped onions
- 2 cloves garlic, minced
- 5 cups beef bone broth, homemade (here) or store-bought
- 1 medium tomato, diced
- ¼ cup chopped fresh cilantro leaves
- 2 tablespoons lime juice Lime wedges, for garnish

Directions

1.   Preheat the oven to 350°F.

2.   Make the meatballs: Put the ground beef, mushrooms, onions, garlic, jalapeño, salt, cumin, and egg in a bowl. Work everything together with your hands.

3.   Shape the meat mixture into 1-inch balls and place on a rimmed baking sheet. Bake for 15 minutes or until cooked through.

4.   Meanwhile, heat the lard in a large saucepan over medium-high heat. Add the onions and sauté for 3 minutes or until soft. Add the garlic and sauté for 1 minute

more. Add the broth, tomato, and cilantro, bring to a boil, and boil for 4 minutes. Reduce the heat and simmer until the meatballs are done baking.

5.   Just before serving, stir in the lime juice and add the meatballs. Taste and add more salt, if desired. Ladle the soup into bowls and serve with lime wedges.

6.   The soup is best served fresh, but leftovers can be stored in an airtight container in the refrigerator for up to 5 days or frozen in a freezer-safe container for up to a month. To reheat, place the soup in a saucepan over medium heat for a few minutes, until warmed through.

Nutritional Information: Calories: 309, Carbs: 3g, Fat: 23g, Fiber: 1g, Protein: 21g

Stuffed-Pepper Soup (One Pot)

Serves: 8

Preparation time: 20 minutes

Cooking time: 1 hours

Ingredients

- 4 tablespoons olive oil, divided
- 1-pound ground beef
- 4 cups bone broth
- 1 (12-ounce) can tomato sauce
- 1 (12-ounce) bag riced cauliflower
- 1 (3.8-ounce) can diced black olives, drained
- 2 green bell peppers, diced
- 3 tablespoons minced garlic

Directions

1. In a large pot, heat 2 tablespoons of oil over medium-high heat. Add the beef and cook, stirring, until browned, about 5 minutes.

2. Add the broth, tomato sauce, cauliflower, olives, peppers, and garlic, and bring to a simmer.

3. Reduce the heat to low and let simmer for about 1 hour, or until the soup is thickened and the flavors have melded. Serve hot.

Nutritional Information: Calories: 286, Carbs: 8g, Fat: 18g, Fiber: 3g, Protein: 23g

Broccoli Salad (One Pot)

Serves: 6

Preparation time: 10 minutes

Ingredients

- 1 (12-ounce) bag broccoli slaw (or 1 head broccoli, chopped or shredded)
- 1½ cups low-carb mayonnaise (like Primal Kitchen)
- 6 tablespoons salted sunflower seeds
- ½ cup chopped red onion
- ¼ cup white vinegar
- 4 strips Perfect Bacon, chopped
- 2 teaspoons Swerve granular (or another granulated alternative sweetener)
- 5 red grapes (optional)

Directions

1. In an airtight container, mix the broccoli slaw, mayonnaise, sunflower seeds, onion, vinegar, bacon, sweetener, and grapes (if using).

2. Cover and chill for at least 2 hours. Serve cold. Store in an airtight container in the refrigerator for up to 3 days.

Nutritional Information: Calories: 564, Carbs: 7g, Fat: 56g, Fiber: 2g, Protein: 7g

Chilled Tomato and Ham Soup

Serves: 6

Preparation time: 5 minutes plus 15 minutes to chill

Ingredients

- ¾ pound plum tomatoes, quartered
- 1 clove garlic, whacked with the side of a large knife and peeled
- ¼ cup avocado oil
- 1 tablespoon coconut vinegar, plus more for serving
- Fine sea salt and ground black pepper
- 4 thin slices prosciutto (about 1 ounce), sliced into strips about ¼ inch wide
- Fresh herbs of choice, for garnish (optional)

Directions

1. Place the tomatoes, garlic, oil, and vinegar in a blender or food processor and pulse until smooth. Season with salt and pepper and refrigerate for about 15 minutes, until cold.

2. Press the eggs through a sieve or colander with tiny holes.

3. Ladle the chilled soup into bowls and drizzle a little vinegar and oil on top. Serve the soup topped with the sieved hard-boiled eggs and strips of ham. Garnish with fresh herbs, if desired.

4. Store in an airtight container in the refrigerator for up to 3 days. To reheat, place the soup in a saucepan over medium heat for a few minutes, until warmed through.

Nutritional Information: Calories: 406, Carbs: 8g, Fat: 36g, Fiber: 2g, Protein: 15g

Rainbow Chopped Salad (One Pot)

Serves: 1

Preparation time: 20 minutes

Ingredients

· 1 cup chopped romaine lettuce

· 1 avocado, halved, pitted, peeled, and diced

· 2 No-Fail Hard-Boiled Eggs, chopped

· ½ cup diced Perfect Bacon

· 10 blueberries

· 4 small cherry tomatoes, halved

· 1 radish, chopped

· 1 breast of Slow-Cooker Buffalo Chicken (optional)

· ¼ cup low-carb, dairy-free ranch dressing (such as Tessemae's)

Directions

1. In a medium bowl, combine the lettuce, avocado, eggs, bacon, blueberries, cherry tomatoes, and radish. Add the chicken (if using) and salad dressing, toss to combine, and serve immediately.

Nutritional Information: Calories: 864, Carbs: 23g, Fat: 73g, Fiber: 13g, Protein: 35g

Chinese Beef and Broccoli Soup

Serves: 8

Preparation time: 10 minutes

Cooking time: 18 minutes

Ingredients

- 2 pounds cubed beef stew meat
- 1 tablespoon wheat-free tamari, or
- ¼ cup coconut aminos
- 2 tablespoons plus
- 2 teaspoons coconut oil, divided
- 1 cup diced onions
- 5 cloves garlic, minced
- 1 tablespoon peeled and grated fresh ginger (optional)
- ¼ teaspoon fine sea salt
- ½ teaspoon ground black pepper
- 6 cups broccoli florets, cut into bite-sized pieces
- 6 cups beef bone broth
- 2 tablespoons fish sauce
- 2 tablespoons Swerve confectioners
- Scallions, sliced diagonally, for garnish

Directions

1.	If any of the stew meat pieces are larger than about 1 inch, cut them down to size. Place the meat in a medium-sized bowl.

2.	Add the tamari and toss to coat. Place in the refrigerator to marinate for at least 1 hour or overnight.

3.	Heat 1 tablespoon of coconut oil in a large pot or Dutch oven over medium-high heat. When the oil is rippling hot, add half of the beef. Spread the beef across the pot and cook, without stirring, for 1 minute. Stir or toss with tongs, spread the beef across the pot again, and cook for 1 minute more. Be careful not to overcook the meat; it should be just barely cooked through and still very tender. Transfer the meat to a dish with a lid.

4.   Drain any excess liquid from the pot. Repeat Step 2 with another tablespoon of coconut oil and the remaining meat.

5.   Add the second batch of cooked meat and any juices from the pot to the dish and cover tightly with the lid.

6.   Add the remaining 2 teaspoons of coconut oil and the onions, garlic, and ginger, if using, to the hot pot. Toss to coat the onions with the oil, sprinkle with the salt and pepper, and cook for about 5 minutes, stirring occasionally, until the onions are tender.

7.   Add the broccoli and beef broth and bring to a simmer. Stir in the fish sauce and sweetener and taste; add more salt or sweetener, if desired. Simmer for 4 minutes or until the broccoli is soft.

8.   Remove from the heat and stir in the cooked meat and any juices. Ladle the soup into bowls, garnish with sliced scallions, and serve.

9.   Store in an airtight container in the refrigerator for up to 3 days. To reheat, place the soup in a saucepan over medium heat for a few minutes, until warmed through.

Nutritional Information: Calories: 426, Carbs: 7g, Fat: 28g, Fiber: 4g, Protein: 35g

Turkey and Orzo Soup

Serves: 8

Preparation time: 10 minutes

Cooking time: 18 minutes

Ingredients

· 1 tablespoon coconut oil

· 2 tablespoons finely diced onions

· 2 cups coarsely chopped cauliflower florets

· 6 cups chicken bone broth, homemade or store-bought

· 1½ cups diced roasted turkey or chicken

· Fine sea salt (optional)

· 3 tablespoons chopped fresh dill, plus extra for garnish

· Freshly ground black pepper, for garnish

Directions

1. Melt the coconut oil in a Dutch oven or stockpot over medium-high heat. Add the onions and sauté for 4 minutes or until translucent. Add the cauliflower and sauté for another 3 minutes. Add the broth, turkey, and dill and simmer for 3 minutes or until heated through. Taste and add salt, if needed.

2. Ladle the soup into bowls and garnish with a sprig of dill and some freshly ground pepper before serving.

3. Store in an airtight container in the refrigerator for up to 3 days. To reheat, place the soup in a saucepan over medium heat for a few minutes, until warmed through.

Nutritional Information: Calories: 179, Carbs: 17g, Fat: 18g, Fiber: 2g, Protein: `8g

Coconut Ginger Chicken Soup

Serves: 8

Preparation time: 10 minutes

Cooking time: 50 minutes

Ingredients

· ¼ cup peeled and grated fresh ginger

· 3 cloves garlic, chopped

· 4 stalks lemongrass, hard outer layers removed and top third discarded, then chopped

· 3 shallots, chopped

· 1 teaspoon ground white pepper

· 4 cups full-fat coconut milk

· 4 boneless, skinless chicken breast halves (about 2 pounds), chopped into bite-sized pieces

· Grated zest of 2 limes

· 3 tablespoons fish sauce

· 5 serrano chile peppers, minced (seeded for less heat)

· ½ teaspoon fine sea salt

Directions

1. Make the ginger paste: Place the ginger and garlic in a food processor or mortar and pulse or pound (using the pestle) into a paste. Add the lemongrass, shallots, and white pepper and pulverize. Set aside.

2. In a medium-sized saucepan, bring the coconut milk to a gentle simmer over medium heat. Do not overheat or it will curdle. Add the ginger paste and stir well, then add the chicken and bring to a boil. Add the lime zest, fish sauce, chiles, and salt. Cover and simmer over medium-low heat for about 45 minutes, until the chicken is fully cooked.

3. Ladle the soup into bowls, then garnish with chives, cilantro, and lime wedges and serve.

4.   Store in an airtight container in the refrigerator for up to 3 days. To reheat, place the soup in a saucepan over medium heat for a few minutes, until warmed through.

Nutritional Information: Calories: 441, Carbs: 7g, Fat: 27g, Fiber: 1g, Protein: 39g

Manhattan Clam Chowder

Serves: 4

Preparation time: 8 minutes

Cooking time: 20 minutes

Ingredients

· 4 strips bacon, diced

· ¼ cup diced onions

· 2 cloves garlic, minced

· 1 stalk celery, diced

· 1 green bell pepper, diced

· 1 small zucchini, diced

· ½ teaspoon dried thyme leaves

· 1 teaspoon fine sea salt

· ½ teaspoon ground black pepper

· 1 large tomato, diced, with juices

· 2 tablespoons tomato paste

· 4 cups chicken bone broth, homemade or store-bought

· 1 (8-ounce) bottle clam juice

· 2 bay leaves

· 2 (10-ounce) cans baby clams with liquid

For Garnish

· Avocado oil or extra-virgin olive oil

· Chopped fresh parsley, oregano, or other herb of choice

Directions

1.   Sauté the bacon in a stockpot or Dutch oven over medium-high heat until crisp, about 4 minutes.

2.   Add the onions and garlic to the pot and sauté for 2 minutes, then add the celery, bell pepper, zucchini, and thyme. Season the veggies with the salt and pepper and sauté for 4 more minutes.

3.   Add the tomato, tomato paste, broth, clam juice, and bay leaves. Bring to a boil, then lower the heat and simmer for 10 minutes.

4.   Just before serving, add the clams and cook just until the clams are warmed through. Taste and add more seasoning, if desired. Ladle the soup into bowls and garnish with a drizzle of oil and parsley leaves.

5.   Store in an airtight container in the refrigerator for up to 3 days. To reheat, place the soup in a saucepan over medium heat for a few minutes, until warmed through.

Nutritional Information: Calories: 306, Carbs: 13g, Fat: 14g, Fiber: 3g, Protein: 14g

Wedge Salad with Ranch Dressing (One Pot)

Serves: 4

Preparation time: 20 minutes

Ingredients

·   1 head iceberg lettuce, cut into 4 wedges

·   ½ cup low-carb, dairy-free ranch dressing (such as Tessemae's)

·   6 tablespoons bacon bits

·   1 tomato, diced

·   4 radishes, diced

·   ¼ cup chopped fresh chives

·   ½ teaspoon freshly ground black pepper

Directions

1.   Arrange the lettuce wedges on 4 serving plates. Top each wedge with 2 tablespoons of dressing. Add the bacon bits, tomato, radishes, chives, and pepper. Serve immediately.

Nutritional Information: Calories: 201, Carbs: 6g, Fat: 17g, Fiber: 1g, Protein: 6g

Cold Cauliflower "Pasta" Salad

Serves: 8

Preparation time: 15 minutes

Ingredients

· 2 (12-ounce) bags riced cauliflower

· 1 red bell pepper, seeded and diced

· 1 cup diced dried salami

· 1 cucumber, diced

· ¼ cup olive oil

· 2 tablespoons minced garlic

· 1 teaspoon salt

Directions

1. In the microwave, cook the cauliflower rice according to the package directions. Refrigerate for at least 30 minutes.

2. Add the bell pepper, salami, cucumber, olive oil, garlic, and salt. Mix well, then cover and refrigerate for at least 2 hours to chill.

3. Serve cold or store in an airtight container in the refrigerator for up to 1 week.

Nutritional Information: Calories: 208, Carbs: 7g, Fat: 16g, Fiber: 3g, Protein: 9g

Egg Salad with Dill (One Pot)

Serves: 12

Preparation time: 15 minutes

Ingredients

·   12 No-Fail Hard-Boiled Eggs, peeled and diced

·   1½ cups low-carb mayonnaise (such as Primal Kitchen)

·   1 teaspoon salt

·   1 teaspoon chopped fresh dill

·   1 teaspoon Swerve granular (or another granulated alternative sweetener)

·   ½ teaspoon freshly ground black pepper

·   ½ teaspoon paprika

Directions

1.   In a medium bowl, combine the eggs, mayonnaise, salt, dill, sweetener, pepper, and paprika.

2.   Cover and refrigerate for at least 2 hours. Serve cold. Store in an airtight container in the refrigerator for up to 1 week.

Nutritional Information: Calories: 280, Carbs: 1g, Fat: 28g, Fiber: 0g, Protein: 6g

Smoky Spicy Chicken Stew

Serves: 12

Preparation time: 7 minutes

Cooking time: 16 minutes

Ingredients

- 1 tablespoon lard or coconut oil
- 2 pounds ground chicken
- 2 boneless, skinless chicken thighs, cut into ½-inch dice
- 1 cup chopped onions
- 3 tablespoons minced garlic
- 2 tablespoons smoked paprika
- 1 tablespoon ground cumin
- 1 tablespoon dried oregano leaves
- 2 teaspoons fine sea salt
- 1 teaspoon cayenne pepper
- 1 (28-ounce) can diced tomatoes, with juices
- 2 cups chicken bone broth, homemade or store-bought
- 1 (12-ounce) can lime-flavored sparkling water or seltzer water
- 1-ounce unsweetened baking chocolate, finely chopped
- ¼ cup lime juice
- ¼ cup chopped fresh cilantro

For Garnish
- Chopped fresh cilantro
- Lime wedges or slices
- Crushed red pepper

Directions

1.   Combine the lard, ground chicken, diced chicken thighs, and onions in a large soup pot over medium-high heat. Cook until the onions are soft and the chicken is cooked through, about 6 minutes.

2.   Add the garlic, paprika, cumin, oregano, salt, and cayenne to the pot and sauté for another minute, while stirring. Add the tomatoes with juices, broth, sparkling water, and chocolate. Simmer gently for 10 minutes to allow the flavors to develop.

3.   Just before serving, stir in the lime juice and cilantro. Garnish with additional cilantro, lime wedges or slices, and some crushed red pepper, if desired.

4.   Store in an airtight container in the refrigerator for up to 3 days. To reheat, place the stew in a saucepan over medium heat for 5 minutes or until warmed through.

Nutritional Information: Calories: 278, Carbs: 6g, Fat: 16g, Fiber: 2g, Protein: 26g

Italian Orzo Soup

Serves: 4

Preparation time: 5 minutes

Cooking time: 18 minutes

Ingredients

·   2 tablespoons coconut oil or lard

·   1 cup diced onions

·   1 cup diced celery

·   3 cloves garlic, minced

·   2 teaspoons Italian seasoning

·   8 large eggs

·   4 cups chicken bone broth, homemade (here) or store-bought, divided

·   ½ teaspoon fine sea salt

·   ½ teaspoon ground black pepper

·   1 cup chunky marinara sauce or diced fire-roasted tomatoes

·   1 cup fresh basil leaves

·   Crushed red pepper or freshly ground black pepper, for garnish

Directions

1.   Heat the coconut oil in a stockpot over medium-high heat. Add the onions and celery and sauté until the onions are translucent, about 3 minutes. Add the garlic and Italian seasoning and sauté for another minute.

2.   In a bowl, whisk the eggs with ¼ cup of the broth and the salt and pepper. Pour the whisked egg mixture into the pot and use a whisk to cook the eggs into a rice like consistency, scraping the bottom of the pot to deglaze, about 3 minutes.

3.   Add the remaining 3¾ cups of the broth and the marinara sauce. Simmer over medium heat for 6 to 8 minutes to develop the flavors.

4.   Just before serving, add the basil leaves and cook for 2 minutes or until the basil is just getting soft. Taste and add more salt, if desired. Ladle the soup into bowls. Garnish with crushed red pepper or freshly ground black pepper and serve.

5.	Store in an airtight container in the refrigerator for up to 4 days. To reheat, place the soup in a saucepan over medium heat for 4 minutes or until warmed through.

Nutritional Information: Calories: 341, Carbs: 9g, Fat: 26g, Fiber: 2g, Protein: 26g

Simple Ham Salad (One Pot)

Serves: 4

Preparation time: 10 minutes

Ingredients

- 2 cups diced ham
- ¾ cup low-carb mayonnaise (such as Primal Kitchen)
- 2 celery stalks, diced

Directions

1. In a small bowl, combine the ham, mayonnaise, and celery, and stir to mix well. Serve immediately or store, covered, in the refrigerator for up to 1 week.

Nutritional Information: Calories: 434, Carbs: 3g, Fat: 42g, Fiber: 1g, Protein: 11g

Thai Red Curry Shrimp Soup

Serves: 4

Preparation time: 5 minutes

Cooking time: 25-45 minutes

Ingredients

· 1 tablespoon avocado oil or coconut oil

· 1-pound medium shrimp, peeled and deveined

· Fine sea salt and ground black pepper

· 3 shallots, finely diced

· 1½ cups chicken bone broth, homemade or store-bought

· 1 (13½-ounce) can full-fat coconut milk

· 1½ tablespoons red curry paste

· ¼ cup fresh cilantro leaves

· ¼ cup scallion pieces (about ½ inch long)

· Juice of 1 lime

For Garnish

· Sliced scallions

· Fresh cilantro leaves Lime wedges

Directions

1.   Heat the oil in a large cast-iron skillet over medium heat. Season the shrimp with salt and pepper and sauté for 2 minutes or until cooked through. Remove from the pan and set aside.

2.   Add the shallots and sauté until tender, about 2 minutes. Reduce the heat to low. Whisk in the broth, coconut milk, and curry paste. Simmer, uncovered, stirring often, for 10 minutes or until the broth has reduced a bit. The longer you simmer, the thicker your sauce will be.

3.   Stir in the cilantro, scallions, and lime juice. Return the shrimp to the pan and stir to coat in the sauce. Immediately remove the pan from the heat and ladle the soup into bowls. Garnish with sliced scallions, cilantro leaves, and lime wedges.

4.   Store in an airtight container in the refrigerator for up to 4 days. To reheat, place the soup in a saucepan over medium heat for 4 minutes or until warmed through.

Nutritional Information: Calories: 362, Carbs: 6g, Fat: 23g, Fiber: 1g, Protein: 32g

Chicken Salad with Grapes and Almonds

Serves: 8

Preparation time: 20 minutes

Ingredients

· 6 boneless, skinless chicken breasts

· 3 tablespoons olive oil

· 1½ cups sugar-free mayonnaise (such as Primal Kitchen)

· ½ cup diced celery

· 10 grapes, diced (optional)

· ¼ cup slivered almonds

· 3 tablespoons poppy seeds

· 1 tablespoon chopped fresh dill

· 1 tablespoon dry mustard

Directions

1. Place the chicken breasts in a stockpot and cover completely with water. Bring to a boil and cook until the chicken is cooked through. about 20 minutes. Drain.

2. Put the chicken in a blender or food processor with the olive oil. Pulse until the chicken is very finely chopped.

3. In a large bowl, combine the chicken with the mayonnaise, celery, grapes (if using), almonds, poppy seeds, dill, and mustard. Serve immediately or cover and refrigerate for up to 1 week.

Nutritional Information: Calories: 506, Carbs: 2g, Fat: 46g, Fiber: 1g, Protein: 21g

Ham and Fauxtato Soup

Serves: 8

Preparation time: 5 minutes

Cooking time: 15 minutes

Ingredients

- 3½ cups chopped cauliflower florets
- ⅓ cup diced celery
- ⅓ cup finely chopped onions
- ¾ cup diced cooked ham
- 3¼ cups chicken bone broth, homemade or store-bought
- ½ teaspoon sea salt
- 1 teaspoon ground black pepper
- 5 tablespoons Kite Hill brand cream cheese style spread

Directions

1.   Combine the cauliflower, celery, onions, ham, broth, salt, and pepper in a stockpot. Bring to a boil, then cover and cook over medium heat until the cauliflower is tender, 10 to 15 minutes.

2.   Remove from the heat and scoop about half of the hot soup into a blender or food processor. Add the cream cheese spread and pulse until very smooth. Return the puree to the pot and stir to combine. Taste and add more salt and pepper, if desired. Ladle the soup into bowls and serve immediately.

3.   Store in an airtight container in the refrigerator for up to 4 days or freeze in a freezer-safe container for up to a month. To reheat, place the soup in a saucepan over medium heat for 4 minutes or until warmed through.

Nutritional Information: Calories: 118, Carbs: 4g, Fat: 8g, Fiber: 1g, Protein: 7g

Salmon Soup

Serves: 8

Preparation time: 10 minutes

Cooking time: 20 minutes

Ingredients

· 1 tablespoon avocado oil or coconut oil

· ¼ cup thinly sliced red onions

· 2 tablespoons minced garlic

· 1-pound skinned salmon fillets, cut into 1-inch chunks

· 1 large tomato, seeded and coarsely chopped

· 1 tablespoon fish sauce

· ¼ teaspoon fine sea salt

· 4 cups fish or chicken bone broth, homemade or store-bought

· 3 tablespoons chopped fresh dill

For Garnish:

· Sprigs of fresh dill Capers

· Sliced fresh chives (optional)

· Freshly ground black pepper

Directions

1. Heat the oil in a saucepan over medium heat. Add the onions and cook for 4 minutes or until soft, stirring occasionally. Add the garlic and sauté for another minute or until fragrant.

2. Add the salmon, tomato, fish sauce (if using), salt, and broth. Bring to a boil over high heat, then reduce the heat to low and simmer gently for 12 minutes or until the salmon is cooked through. Serve immediately, garnished with sprigs of fresh dill, capers, chives (if using), and freshly ground pepper.

3. Store in an airtight container in the refrigerator for up to 3 days. To reheat, place in a saucepan over medium heat for 5 minutes or until warmed through.

Nutritional Information: Calories: 259, Carbs: 4g, Fat: 14g, Fiber: 1g, Protein: 27g

Chicken and Rice Soup

Serves: 8

Preparation time: 5 minutes

Cooking time: 20 minutes

Ingredients

· 6 large eggs, beaten

· 8 cups chicken bone broth, homemade or store-bought, divided

· ½ teaspoon fine sea salt

· ½ teaspoon ground black pepper

· 2 tablespoons lard or coconut oil

· 1 cup diced onions

· 1 cup diced celery

· 4 boneless, skinless chicken thighs, cut into ½-inch

· 2 sprigs fresh thyme, or 1 teaspoon dried thyme leaves

· 1 bay leaf

· 2 tablespoons lime juice

For Garnish

· Fresh thyme sprigs

· Extra-virgin olive oil

Directions

1. In a medium-sized bowl, combine the eggs, ¼ cup of the broth, salt, and pepper.

2. Heat the lard in a stockpot over medium-high heat. Add the onions and sauté for 3 minutes or until soft.

3. Add the celery and cook for another 2 minutes. Add the egg mixture and use a whisk to deglaze the bottom of the pot as the eggs cook, about 3 minutes. Whisk continuously to create small pieces that resemble rice.

4.   Add the remaining broth, chicken, thyme, and bay leaf to the pot. Boil for 10 minutes or until the chicken is cooked through and no longer pink. Discard the bay leaf and stir in the lime juice. Taste and adjust the seasoning to your liking.

5.   Ladle the soup into bowls. Garnish with thyme leaves and a drizzle of olive oil, if desired.

6.   Store in an airtight container in the refrigerator for up to 3 days. To reheat, place the soup in a saucepan over medium heat for 4 minutes or until warmed through.

Nutritional Information: Calories: 223, Carbs: 4g, Fat: 14g, Fiber: 1g, Protein: 20g

Spicy Shrimp Salad (One Pot)

Serves: 8

Preparation time: 10 minutes

Ingredients

- 3 dozen shrimp, cooked and peeled
- ¼ cup avocado oil
- 1 tablespoon chopped fresh cilantro
- 1 teaspoon cayenne
- 1 teaspoon garlic salt
- 1 teaspoon freshly ground black pepper

Directions

1. In a large bowl, mix together the shrimp, avocado oil, cilantro, cayenne, garlic salt, and pepper.

2. Serve immediately or store in an airtight container in the refrigerator for up to 5 days.

Nutritional Information: Calories: 561, Carbs: 5g, Fat: 44g, Fiber: 1g, Protein: 37g

Salad Kabobs

Serves: 4

Preparation time: 7 minutes

Ingredients

· ½ head iceberg lettuce, cut into 1-inch squares

· 8 hard-boiled eggs, peeled and halved

· 1 pound sliced or cubed ham

· 1 cup pitted black olives

· 1 cup cherry tomatoes

· ½ cup dairy-free ranch dressing, homemade or store-bought, for serving

Directions

1. Thread a few squares of lettuce onto a skewer. Add a slice of ham folded twice to form a square or cube, an olive, a few more squares of lettuce, a tomato, another cube of ham, a few more squares of lettuce, and an egg half.

2. Place the kabob on a platter and repeat with the remaining ingredients and skewers. Serve with a bowl of dressing for dipping.

3. These kabobs are best served fresh; however, you can store the ka-bobs and dressing in separate airtight containers in the refrigerator for up to 2 days.

Nutritional Information: Calories: 373, Carbs: 5g, Fat: 31g, Fiber: 1g, Protein: 19g

Asparagus Cobb Salad

Serves: 8

Preparation time: 8 minutes

Cooking time: 20 minutes

Ingredients

· 1-pound asparagus, ends trimmed

· 2 tablespoons melted lard, tallow, or coconut oil

· ½ teaspoon fine sea salt

· ¼ teaspoon ground black pepper

· 5 cloves garlic, minced

· 2 tablespoons chopped fresh chives, plus extra for garnish

· 1 cup diced ham

· 2 hard-boiled eggs, peeled and chopped (omit for egg-free)

· ¼ cup dairy-free ranch dressing, homemade or store-bought

Directions

1.   Preheat the oven to 400°F.

2.   Place the asparagus on a rimmed baking sheet. Drizzle with the melted lard and season with the salt and pepper. Turn the asparagus in the fat to coat evenly, then spread the spears out in a single layer. Top with the garlic and chives.

3.   Roast the asparagus until slightly charred on the ends, 10 minutes for thin spears or 20 minutes for medium to thick spears.

4.   Transfer the asparagus to a platter and top with the ham, eggs, and dressing. Garnish with additional chives.

5.   This salad is best served fresh; however, you can store the salad and dressing in separate airtight containers in the refrigerator for up to 4 days.

Nutritional Information: Calories: 336, Carbs: 6g, Fat: 26g, Fiber: 0g, Protein: 19g

Crab Louie Salad

Serves: 4

Preparation time: 6 minutes

Cooking time: 3 minutes

Ingredients

- 4 strips bacon, diced
- 1 head romaine lettuce, chopped
- 8 ounces canned crabmeat
- 4 hard-boiled eggs, peeled and quartered (omit for egg-free)
- 1 tomato, diced
- ¼ cup diced red onions
- ½ cup sliced black olives
- ¾ cup Crab Louie Dressing, for serving
- Freshly ground black pepper, for garnish

Directions

1. Fry the bacon in a skillet over medium heat, stirring often, until slightly crisp, about 3 minutes. Remove from the skillet and set aside on a paper towel–lined plate to drain and cool.

2. Make a bed of romaine lettuce on a platter. Top with a row each of egg quarters, tomatoes, onions, cooked bacon, crabmeat, and olives. Drizzle with the dressing and garnish with freshly ground pepper.

3. Store the salad and dressing in separate airtight containers in the refrigerator for up to 4 days.

Nutritional Information: Calories: 402, Carbs: 6g, Fat: 31g, Fiber: 1g, Protein: 22g

Chapter Six: Poultry Recipes

Slow-Cooker Buffalo Chicken

Serves: 8

Preparation time: 10 minutes

Cooking time: 4 hours

Ingredients

· 6 boneless, skinless chicken breasts

· 1 cup hot wing sauce (such as Frank's Red-hot)

· 1 (8-ounce) container dairy-free cream cheese (such as Kite Hill)

· 1 onion, diced (optional)

· ¼ cup olive oil

Directions

1. In the slow cooker, combine the chicken, hot sauce, cream cheese, onion (if using), and olive oil. Cover and cook on low for 7 hours or on high for 4 hours.

2. Once cooked, transfer the chicken breasts to a cutting board and use two forks to shred the meat. Return the meat to the sauce in the pot.

3. Serve hot, as a dip, with a side, or straight from the bowl.

Nutritional Information: Calories: 218, Carbs: 1g, Fat: 14g, Fiber: 0g, Protein: 22g

Salt-And-Pepper Chicken Kebabs with Pineapple

Serves: 6

Preparation time: 15 minutes

Cooking time: 30 minutes

Ingredients

- 6 boneless, skinless chicken breasts, cut into
- 2-inch pieces
- ¼ cup olive oil, plus
- 2 tablespoons more for greasing the skewers
- 2 teaspoons salt
- 1 teaspoon freshly ground black pepper
- 12 (2-inch) chunks pineapple
- 1 green bell pepper, seeded and cut into squares
- 1 onion, cut into 2-inch pieces
- 8 ounces whole mushrooms

Directions

1. Preheat the oven to 400°F.

2. In a large bowl, toss the chicken pieces with the olive oil, salt, and pepper.

3. Grease 6 metal skewers with olive oil (so the chicken will be easier to remove when you eat it later). Thread the pineapple, chicken, pepper, onion, and mushrooms onto the skewers, starting and ending each skewer with pineapple.

4. Lay the skewers on a large rimmed baking sheet and cover with the remaining 2 tablespoons oil. Bake for 30 minutes, or until browned and cooked through.

Nutritional Information: Calories: 293, Carbs: 7g, Fat: 17g, Fiber: 3g, Protein: 28g

Umami Chicken Burgers

Serves: 4

Preparation time: 10 minutes

Cooking time: 20 minutes

Ingredients

·   5 tablespoons olive oil, divided

·   12 ounces spinach

·   1-pound ground chicken

·   ¼ cup fish sauce (I like Red Boat; see tip)

Directions

1.   Heat 3 tablespoons of olive oil in a large skillet over medium heat. Add the spinach and sauté until wilted, about 2 minutes. Transfer the spinach to a medium bowl and let cool.

2.   Once the spinach has cooled, add the chicken and fish sauce to it, and mix well with your hands. Form the mixture into 4 patties.

3.   Heat the remaining 2 tablespoons of olive oil in the skillet over medium heat. Add the meat patties to the skillet and cook for about 4 minutes per side, or until browned and cooked through. Serve immediately or wrap and refrigerate for up to 1 week.

Nutritional Information: Calories: 351, Carbs: 4g, Fat: 27g, Fiber: 2g, Protein: 23g

Best Fried Chicken Ever

Serves: 4-6

Preparation time: 3 hours

Cooking time: 30 to 40 minutes

Ingredients

· 8 to 10 boneless, skin-on chicken thighs or boneless, skinless breasts (or a combo)

· 1 cup dill pickle juice

· ¾ cup almond flour

· 2 tablespoons minced garlic

· 2 teaspoons freshly ground black pepper

· 2 teaspoons paprika

· 1½ teaspoons salt

· 1 teaspoon dry mustard

· ¾ cup olive oil

Directions

1. In a large bowl or plastic bag, combine the chicken with the pickle juice and refrigerate for at least 3 hours or, ideally, overnight.

2. In a large bowl, combine the almond flour, garlic, pepper, paprika, salt, and dry mustard.

3. Heat the oil in a large skillet over medium-high heat.

4. While the oil is heating, remove the chicken from the marinade, shaking off any excess and discarding the marinade. Coat each piece of chicken in the flour mixture. Add the coated chicken to the skillet. Reduce the heat to medium-low and cook the chicken, turning it every 5 minutes or so, until it's browned and crispy, about 20 minutes.

5. Transfer the chicken to a paper towel–lined plate to drain. Serve hot.

Nutritional Information: Calories: 524, Carbs: 6g, Fat: 44g, Fiber: 3g, Protein: 26g

Chicken and Asparagus Curry

Serves: 4

Preparation time: 5 minutes

Cooking time: 15 minutes

Ingredients

- 1 tablespoon coconut oil
- ½ cup chopped onions
- 1 cinnamon stick
- 2 teaspoons ground fenugreek
- 2 teaspoons dry mustard
- 1 teaspoon ground cumin
- 2 boneless, skinless chicken thighs, cut into ½-inch pieces
- Fine sea salt and ground black pepper
- 1-pound asparagus, trimmed and cut into 2-inch pieces
- 1 (13½-ounce) can full-fat coconut milk
- ¼ cup chicken bone broth, homemade or store-bought
- 2 teaspoons Swerve confectioners'-style sweetener
- ½ teaspoon turmeric powder
- 1 tablespoon red curry paste
- Juice of 1 lime Fresh cilantro leaves, for garnish
- Lime wedges, for serving

Directions

1. Heat the oil in a cast-iron skillet over medium-high heat. Add the onions, cinnamon stick, fenugreek, dry mustard, and cumin and cook for 4 minutes or until the onions are soft.

2. Meanwhile, pat the chicken dry and season well on all sides with salt and pepper. Place in the skillet and cook for 5 minutes on each side, until the chicken is golden brown and no longer pink inside.

3.   Add the asparagus, coconut milk, broth, sweetener, turmeric, curry paste, and lime juice. Stir well to combine. Bring to a simmer, then continue to simmer for 5 minutes or until the asparagus is cooked to your liking. Remove from the heat. Garnish with cilantro and serve with lime wedges.

4.   Store in an airtight container in the refrigerator for up to 3 days. To reheat, place the curry in a saucepan over medium heat for a few minutes, until warmed to your liking.

Nutritional Information: Calories: 313, Carbs: 9g, Fat: 24g, Fiber: 3g, Protein: 15g

Chicken Tinga

Serves: 4

Preparation time: 10 minutes

Cooking time: 40 minutes

Ingredients

Chicken

· 1-pound bone-in, skin-on chicken thighs

· ¼ cup chopped onions 1 tablespoon minced garlic

· 1 tablespoon fine sea salt

· ½ tablespoon ground black pepper

· 4 ounces Mexican-style fresh (raw) chorizo, removed from casings

· ½ large white onion, chopped

· 1 clove garlic, minced

· 3 cups chopped tomatoes

· 1 cup husked and chopped tomatillos

· 2 tablespoons pureed chipotle

· 1½ teaspoons fine sea salt

· 1 teaspoon ground black pepper

· ½ teaspoon dried oregano leaves

· 1 sprig fresh marjoram 1 sprig fresh thyme

· ½ cup chicken bone broth, homemade or store-bought

· 1 batch Keto Tortillas (omit for egg-free), or 8 large lettuce leaves, for serving

Directions

1. Place the chicken, onions, garlic, salt, and pepper in a deep saucepan with 5 cups of water. Bring to a boil over high heat, then reduce the heat to medium and simmer for 20 minutes.

2. Remove the chicken to a cutting board. Using 2 forks, remove the chicken from the bones and shred it; discard the bones and set the shredded chicken aside.

3.   Crumble the chorizo into a large cast-iron skillet. Place the skillet over medium heat, add the onion and garlic, and cook, stirring often, until the sausage is cooked through, about 5 minutes. Add the shredded chicken, tomatoes, tomatillos, chipotle, salt, pepper, and herbs. Continue cooking for 5 minutes, then add the chicken broth and cook for 5 more minutes. Remove the marjoram and thyme sprigs. Serve with tortillas or lettuce leaves.

4.   Store in an airtight container in the refrigerator for up to 3 days. To reheat, place the chicken in a saucepan over medium heat for a few minutes, until warmed to your liking.

Nutritional Information: Calories: 506, Carbs: 10g, Fat: 33g, Fiber: 2g, Protein: 41g

Guacamole Lovers' Stuffed Chicken

Serves: 4

Preparation time: 10 minutes

Cooking time: 17 minutes

Ingredients

Guacamole

· 1 avocado, peeled and pitted 1

· ½ tablespoons lime juice, or more to taste

· 1 small plum tomato, diced

· ¼ cup finely diced onions

· 1 small clove garlic, smashed to a paste

· 1½ tablespoons chopped fresh cilantro leaves

· ¼ scant teaspoon fine sea salt

· ¼ scant teaspoon ground cumin

· 4 boneless, skinless chicken breast halves (about 2 pounds), pounded to ¼ inch thick 8 strips thin-cut bacon

For Serving

· Lime wedges Grape tomatoes

· 1 batch Pico de Gallo (optional)

Directions

1. Preheat the oven to 425°F.

2. Make the guacamole: Place the avocado and lime juice in a large bowl and mash until it reaches your desired consistency. Add the tomato, onions, garlic, cilantro, salt, and cumin and stir until well combined. Taste and add more lime juice, if desired. Place in a large resealable plastic bag, squeeze out all the air, and seal shut. (Note: If making the guacamole ahead of time, it will keep in the refrigerator for up to 3 days when stored this way.)

3. Place a chicken breast on a cutting board. Take a sharp knife and, holding it parallel to the chicken, make a 1-inch-wide incision at the top of the breast.

Carefully cut into the breast to form a large pocket, leaving a ½-inch border along the sides and bottom. Repeat with the other 3 chicken breasts.

4. Cut a ¾-inch hole in one corner of the plastic bag with the guaca-mole, then squirt the guacamole into the pockets in the chicken breasts, dividing the guacamole evenly among them.

5. Wrap 2 strips of bacon around each chicken breast and secure the ends with toothpicks. Place the bacon-wrapped chicken on a rimmed baking sheet. Bake until the bacon is crisp and the chicken is cooked through, about 17 minutes. Serve with lime wedges, tomatoes, and pico de gallo, if desired.

6. Store in an airtight container in the refrigerator for up to 3 days. To reheat, place the chicken on a rimmed baking sheet in a preheated 400°F oven for 5 minutes or until warmed through.

Nutritional Information: Calories: 469, Carbs: 10g, Fat: 28g, Fiber: 4g, Protein: 45g

Chicken Meatball Marinara with Bean Sprouts and Broccoli (One Pot)

Serves: 6

Preparation time: 20 minutes

Cooking time: 45 minutes

Ingredients

- 1-pound ground chicken
- ¼ cup olive oil
- 2 cups chopped broccoli
- 1 (24-ounce) jar low-carb marinara sauce (I like Rao's Homemade)
- 1 (12-ounce) bag bean sprouts (see tip)

Directions

1. Form the ground chicken into 12 meatballs.

2. In a large skillet, heat the oil over medium-high heat. Add the meatballs and cook, turning occasionally, until browned, about 8 minutes. Add the broccoli and marinara sauce. Reduce the heat to low, cover, and let simmer for 30 minutes.

3. Add the bean sprouts, increase the heat to medium, and cook, uncovered, for 15 more minutes. Serve hot.

Nutritional Information: Calories: 247, Carbs: 10g, Fat: 15g, Fiber: 4g, Protein: 18g

Garlic Chicken Wings

Serves: 6

Preparation time: 10 minutes

Cooking time: 1 hour

Ingredients

- 24 frozen chicken wings
- 1 cup olive oil
- 6 garlic cloves, minced
- 1½ teaspoons salt
- 1 teaspoon freshly ground black pepper

Directions

1. Preheat the oven to 400°F. Place a baking rack on top of a large baking sheet.

2. In a large bowl, combine the frozen wings with the olive oil, garlic, salt, and pepper.

3. Arrange the chicken pieces on top of the baking rack on the baking sheet. Bake in the preheated oven for 1 hour, or until browned and crisp.

Nutritional Information: Calories: 880, Carbs: 1g, Fat: 76g, Fiber: 0g, Protein: 48g

Black Skillet Chicken Thighs with Artichoke Hearts

Serves: 6

Preparation time: 10 minutes

Cooking time: 50 Minutes

Ingredients

- 6 tablespoons olive oil
- 6 boneless, skin-on chicken thighs
- 1 (14-ounce) can artichoke hearts, drained
- 1 onion, diced
- ½ cup bone broth
- 1 teaspoon salt
- 1 teaspoon freshly ground black pepper
- Juice of 1 lemon

Directions

1. Preheat the oven to 400°F.

2. Heat the olive oil in a large cast iron skillet over medium-high heat. Add the chicken and cook until nicely browned on the bottom, about 4 minutes.

3. Once browned, flip the chicken over and add the artichokes, onion, broth, salt, and pepper.

4. Place the skillet in the preheated oven and cook for 40 minutes, or until the chicken is cooked through.

5. Remove the skillet from the oven and squeeze the lemon juice over the top. Serve hot.

Nutritional Information: Calories: 479, Carbs: 6g, Fat: 39g, Fiber: 4g, Protein: 25g

Sheet Pan BBQ Chicken Breasts

Serves: 8

Preparation time: 8 minutes

Cooking time: 25 Minutes

Ingredients

·   4 boneless, skinless chicken breast halves (about 2 pounds), sliced into 1½ by 4-inch strips

·   ½ cup Simple BBQ Sauce

·   3 firm and barely ripe avocados

·   1 (1-pound) package thin-cut bacon (about 20 strips)

Directions

1.   Preheat the oven to 425F. Line a rimmed baking sheet with parchment paper.

2.   Baste the chicken strips with BBQ sauce.

3.   Peel and pit the avocados, then slice into thick fry shapes. Wrap each slice with a strip of bacon and secure with a toothpick.

4.   Place the chicken and bacon-wrapped avocado slices on the lined baking sheet. Bake for 20 to 25 minutes, until the avocados are tender and the juice of the chicken runs clear when the center of the thickest part is cut and the internal temperature is at least 165°F. 5.

5.   Store in an airtight container in the refrigerator for up to 3 days or in the freezer for up to a month. To reheat, place the chicken and fries on a baking sheet in a preheated 375°F oven for 5 minutes or until warmed through.

Nutritional Information: Calories: 464, Carbs: 7g, Fat: 40g, Fiber: 23g, Protein: 23g

Chicken with Dried Beef

Serves: 12

Preparation time: 20 minutes

Cooking time: 1 hour

Ingredients

- 6 large boneless, skinless chicken breasts, each cut in half
- 1 (2-ounce) jar or can dried beef
- 12 strips bacon
- 1¼ cups bone broth
- 1 (8-ounce) container dairy-free cream cheese with chives (such as Kite Hill)
- 1 celery stalk, diced
- ½ cup canned coconut milk
- 1 teaspoon freshly ground black pepper

Directions

1. Preheat the oven to 375°F.

2. Wrap each piece of chicken with 2 pieces of dried beef, and then with 1 slice of bacon. Arrange the wrapped chicken pieces in a baking dish.

3. In a medium bowl, mix together the broth, cream cheese, celery, coconut milk, and pepper. Pour the mixture over the chicken pieces.

4. Bake, uncovered, in the preheated oven for 1 hour, or until the chicken is cooked through.

Nutritional Information: Calories: 309, Carbs: 2g, Fat: 21g, Fiber: 0g, Protein: 28g

Chili-Garlic Chicken with Broccoli

Serves: 6

Preparation time: 10 minutes

Cooking time: 6 hours

Ingredients

· 6 boneless, skinless chicken breasts (about 1¼ pounds total), cut into bite-size pieces

· 1 head broccoli, chopped

· 8 ounces whole mushrooms

· 1 large onion, diced

· 2 cups bone broth

· ½ cup coconut aminos

· 5 tablespoons chili-garlic sauce

· ¼ cup avocado oil

· 2 tablespoons fish sauce (such as Red Boat)

· 1 teaspoon minced garlic

· ½ teaspoon grated fresh ginger

Directions

1. In a slow cooker, combine the chicken, broccoli, mushrooms, onion, bone broth, coconut aminos, chili-garlic sauce, avocado oil, fish sauce, garlic, and ginger.

2. Cover and cook on low for 6 hours. Serve hot.

Nutritional information: Calories: 244, Carbs: 9g, Fat: 11g, Fiber: 0g, Protein: 29g

Poppy Seed Chicken

Serves: 8

Preparation time: 20 minutes

Cooking time: 45 minutes

Ingredients

- 2 tablespoons olive oil, plus more for greasing the baking dish
- 6 boneless, skinless chicken breasts (about 2 pounds), cooked and shredded
- 1 (8-ounce) container dairy-free cream cheese (such as Kite Hill)
- 1 cup bone broth 8 ounces mushrooms, sliced
- 1 14-ounce can coconut milk
- 2 tablespoons olive oil
- 1½ teaspoons garlic salt
- 2 tablespoons poppy seeds
- ¼cup slivered almonds

Directions

1. Preheat the oven to 350°F. Grease a 9-by-13-inch baking dish.

2. Arrange the shredded chicken in an even layer in the prepared baking dish.

3. In a medium saucepan over low heat, soften the cream cheese, stirring constantly. Once the cheese is melted, stir in the bone broth, mushrooms, coconut milk, olive oil, and garlic salt.

4. Continue cooking on low until the sauce is well combined and thickened. Remove from the heat and stir in the poppy seeds. Immediately pour the sauce over the shredded chicken in the baking dish. Sprinkle the almonds over the top and bake in the preheated oven for 40 minutes, or until bubbly.

Nutritional Information: Calories 374, Carbs: 7g, Fat: 26g, Fiber: 1g, Protein: 29g

Curry Braised Chicken Legs

Serves: 8

Preparation time: 10 minutes

Cooking time: 45 minutes

Ingredients

- ¼ cup avocado oil or coconut oil
- ¼ cup diced onions
- 1 tablespoon peeled and grated fresh ginger
- 1 tablespoon minced garlic
- 1 cup sliced button mushrooms
- 8 chicken legs
- 1 teaspoon fine sea salt
- 1 cup chicken bone broth, homemade or store-bought
- ½ cup full-fat coconut milk
- 2 tablespoons red curry paste
- 2 tablespoons lime juice Sliced scallions, for garnish
- Lime wedges, for serving

Directions

1. Heat the oil in a large cast-iron skillet over medium-high heat. Add the onions and cook for 2 minutes or until soft. Add the ginger and garlic and cook for another minute. Add the mushrooms and sauté until golden brown, about 2 minutes.

2. Season the chicken on all sides with the salt. Place the chicken in the skillet and sear on all sides for about 2 minutes per side, until golden brown. Add the broth, coconut milk, and curry paste and whisk to combine. Cover and cook for 30 to 40 minutes, until the chicken is cooked through and fork-tender; during cooking, lift the lid occasionally and stir to deglaze the bottom of the pan.

3. Stir in the lime juice. Taste and add more salt, if desired. Garnish with scallions and serve with lime wedges.

4.   Store in an airtight container in the refrigerator for up to 3 days or in the freezer for up to a month. To reheat, place the chicken in a skillet over medium heat, cover, and cook until warmed through, about 5 minutes.

Nutritional Information: Calories 363, Carbs: 2g, Fat: 25g, Fiber: 0.5g, Protein: 30g

Chicken and Mushroom Kabobs

Serves: 2

Preparation time: 10 minutes

Cooking time: 12 minutes

Ingredients

Marinade

· ½ cup MCT oil, avocado oil, or extra-virgin olive oil

· 3 tablespoons lime juice

· 1 tablespoon chopped fresh tarragon or parsley

· 1 teaspoon chopped fresh oregano

· 1 teaspoon fine sea salt

· 1 teaspoon ground black pepper

· 3 cloves garlic, minced

· 2 boneless, skinless chicken thighs, cut into ½-inch pieces

· 6 large button mushrooms, cut into quarters

Dipping Sauce:

· ¼ cup mayonnaise, homemade or store-bought

· 1 tablespoon lime juice

· 1 tablespoon sliced fresh chives, or 2 teaspoons dried chives

· Fine sea salt and ground black pepper

Special Equipment

· 6 wood skewers, soaked in water for 15 minutes

Directions

1. Place the ingredients for the marinade in a large bowl and stir to combine. Add the chicken and stir well to coat. Cover and refrigerate for at least 3 hours or overnight.

2. Preheat a grill to high heat. Thread a piece of marinated chicken onto a skewer, followed by a mushroom quarter. Repeat 3 more times to fill the skewer.

Then repeat with the remaining skewers, chicken, and mushrooms. Discard the marinade.

3.   Lightly brush the hot grill grate with oil, then place the kabobs on the grill and cook for 6 minutes. Flip and grill for another 6 minutes or until the chicken is cooked through.

4.   Meanwhile, prepare the dipping sauce: Place the mayonnaise, lime juice, and chives in a small food processor or blender and blend until smooth. Season to taste with salt and pepper.

5.   Place the kabobs on a platter and serve with a bowl of the dipping sauce on the side.

6.   Store leftover kabobs and sauce in separate airtight containers in the refrigerator for up to 4 days; the kabobs can be frozen for up to a month. Reheat the kabobs in a lightly greased skillet for 2 minutes per side or until warmed to your liking.

Nutritional Information: Calories 436, Carbs: 6g, Fat: 36g, Fiber: 0.5g, Protein: 24g

Easy Asian Chicken Legs

Serves: 4

Preparation time: 5 minutes

Cooking time: 35 minutes

Ingredients

· ½ cup chicken bone broth, homemade or store-bought

· ⅓ cup Swerve confectioners

· ⅓ cup wheat-free tamari

· ¼ cup tomato sauce

· 1 tablespoon coconut vinegar or apple cider vinegar

· ¾ teaspoon crushed red pepper

· ¼ teaspoon peeled and grated fresh ginger

· 1 clove garlic, smashed to a paste

· 5 drops orange oil (optional)

· 1-pound bone-in, skin-on chicken legs or thighs

For Garnish:

· 1 lime, quartered

· 1 tablespoon toasted sesame seeds

· 4 scallions, sliced Fresh cilantro leaves

Directions

1.   Preheat the oven to 400°F.

2.   Place the broth, sweetener, tamari, tomato sauce, vinegar, crushed red pepper, ginger, garlic, and orange oil, if using, in a small bowl. Stir well, then pour half of the sauce into another bowl and set aside for serving.

3.   Place the chicken in an 8-inch square baking dish and baste with the other half of the sauce. Cover and bake for 25 minutes. Uncover and bake for another 10 minutes or until the chicken is cooked through and no longer pink inside.

4.   Serve the chicken with the reserved sauce. Garnish with lime quarters, toasted sesame seeds, sliced scallions, and cilantro leaves.

5. Store in an airtight container in the refrigerator for up to 4 days or in the freezer for up to a month. To reheat, place the chicken in a preheated 375°F oven for 10 minutes or until warmed to your liking.

Nutritional Information: Calories 322, Carbs: 6g, Fat: 25g, Fiber: 2g, Protein: 33g

Lemon Pepper Chicken Tender

Serves: 4

Preparation time: 7 minutes

Cooking time: 20 minutes

Ingredients

· ¼ cup avocado oil or melted coconut oil

· 1 tablespoon minced garlic

· 2 lemons, divided

· 4 boneless, skinless chicken breast halves (about 2 pounds), cut into 1-inch-wide strips

· 2 tablespoons lemon pepper seasoning

· 2 teaspoons fine sea salt

· 1 teaspoon black peppercorns, for garnish

· Chopped fresh parsley or oregano, for garnish

Directions

1. Preheat the oven to 400°F.

2. Make the lemon sauce: Place the oil and garlic in a small bowl. Grate the zest of one of the lemons and add 2 teaspoons of the zest to the bowl. Juice the zested lemon and add the juice to the bowl. Stir well.

3. Cut the second lemon into thin slices. Arrange the slices on a rimmed baking sheet or a 13 by 9-inch baking dish.

4. Season all sides of the chicken strips with the lemon pepper seasoning and salt. Place on top of the lemon slices and drizzle with the lemon sauce.

5. Bake for 18 to 20 minutes, until the chicken is no longer pink inside. Serve garnished with peppercorns and fresh parsley.

6. Store in an airtight container in the refrigerator for up to 3 days or in the freezer for up to a month. To reheat, place the chicken on a rimmed baking sheet in a preheated 375°F oven for 5 minutes or until warmed through.

Nutritional Information: Calories 432, Carbs: 6g, Fat: 25g, Fiber: 2g, Protein: 44g

Bundt Pan Chicken

Serves: 8

Preparation time: 7 minutes

Cooking time: 45 minutes

Ingredients

- 2 medium zucchini, sliced ½ inch thick (about 2½ cups)
- ½ small onion, cut into 1-inch pieces
- 1 tablespoon plus 1 teaspoon minced garlic
- 4 teaspoons fine sea salt, divided
- 2 teaspoons ground black pepper, divided
- 4 tablespoons avocado oil or melted lard, duck fat, or bacon fat, divided
- 3 sprigs fresh thyme, divided
- 1 (3-pound) whole chicken

Directions

1. Place all of the oven racks in the lower portion of the oven. (The chicken stands tall and needs a lot of space above it.) Preheat the oven to 425°F.

2. Place the zucchini, onion, and garlic in a medium-sized bowl. Season with 3 teaspoons of the salt and 1½ teaspoons of the pepper. Drizzle with 1 tablespoon of the oil and toss to coat well. Place in the Bundt pan. Top with a thyme sprig.

3. Place a piece of aluminum foil over the hole of the Bundt pan, then place parchment paper over the foil so the food doesn't touch the foil while roasting.

4. Pat the chicken dry and use your hands to rub the remaining 3 tablespoons of oil all over the outside. Season the inside and outside of the chicken well with the remaining teaspoon of salt and remaining ½ teaspoon of pepper. Place the remaining 2 sprigs of thyme inside the cavity.

5. Place the chicken in the middle of the Bundt pan with the neck facing up. Roast in the oven for 45 minutes or until the chicken is cooked through and the juices run clear. Serve with the roasted veggies.

6.   Store in an airtight container in the refrigerator for up to 3 days or in the freezer for up to a month. To reheat, place on a rimmed baking sheet in a preheated 375°F oven for 8 minutes or until warmed through.

Nutritional Information: Calories 445, Carbs: 6g, Fat: 33g, Fiber: 1g, Protein: 33g

Chapter Seven: Beef & Pork Recipes

Dinner Roast with Vegetables (One Pot)

Serves: 8

Preparation time: 15 minutes

Cooking time: 8 to 10 hours

Ingredients

- 1 (3-pound) chuck roast
- 1 bunch radishes (about 12), diced
- 2 cups bone broth
- 5 celery stalks, chopped
- 8 ounces mushrooms, diced
- 1 onion, diced
- ¼ cup coconut aminos
- ½ cup dairy-free ranch dressing (such as Tessemae's)

Directions

1. In a slow cooker, combine the chuck roast, radishes, bone broth, celery, mushrooms, onion, coconut aminos, and ranch dressing.

2. Cover and cook on low for 8 to 10 hours, or until the meat can be easily pulled apart with a fork.

Nutritional Information: Calories 383, Carbs: 4g, Fat: 18g, Fiber: 1g, Protein: 47g

Classic Keto Meat Loaf

Serves: 8

Preparation time: 10 minutes

Cooking time: 1 hour

Ingredients

· Oil, for greasing the baking sheet

· 1-pound ground beef

· ½ onion, diced

· ½ green bell pepper, seeded and diced

· ⅔ cup sugar-free ketchup (such as Primal Kitchen), divided

· 1 large egg

· 1 teaspoon dried sage

· 1 teaspoon dry mustard

· 1 teaspoon salt

· 1 teaspoon freshly ground black pepper

Directions

1. Preheat the oven to 350°F. Grease a large rimmed baking sheet.

2. In a large bowl, mix together the ground beef, onion, green pepper, ⅓ cup of ketchup, the egg, sage, dry mustard, salt, and pepper. Form the mixture into a loaf on the baking sheet, and then top it with the remaining ⅓ cup of ketchup.

3. Cook in the preheated oven for 1 hour. Let rest for 5 to 10 minutes before slicing.

Nutritional Information: Calories 260, Carbs: 3g, Fat: 21g, Fiber: 1g, Protein: 13g

Beef Liver Burgers

Serves: 5

Preparation time: 10 minutes

Cooking time: 20 minutes

Ingredients

- 1-pound ground beef or bison
- 8 ounces beef liver, cut into small pieces
- 3 tablespoons sugar-free ketchup (such as Primal Kitchen)
- 3 teaspoons garlic salt, divided
- 3 tablespoons olive oil

Directions

1.   In a small bowl, combine the ground meat, liver, ketchup, and 2 teaspoons of garlic salt. Mix well and form into 4 to 6 burger patties.

2.   In a cast iron skillet, heat the oil over medium heat. Add the burgers, then sprinkle them with the remaining teaspoon of garlic salt. Cook for 8 to 10 minutes per side, or until cooked through. Serve hot.

Nutritional Information: Calories 497, Carbs: 3g, Fat: 41g, Fiber: 0g, Protein: 30g

Easy BBQ Brisket

Serves: 8

Preparation time: 4 minutes

Cooking time: 4 hours

Ingredients

4 pounds brisket

· 6 tablespoons powdered sweetener

· 2 tablespoons fine sea salt

· 1 tablespoon garlic powder

· 1 tablespoon ground black pepper

· 1 tablespoon onion powder

· 1 tablespoon dry mustard

· 1 ½ cups tomato sauce

· 1 ½ cups beef bone broth, homemade

· 2 teaspoons liquid smoke

· Chopped fresh parsley, for garnish

Directions

1. Pat the brisket dry. Place in a large roasting pan that snugly fits the brisket and allow it to sit at room temperature for 10 to 15 minutes.

2. Preheat oven to 350F,

3. Place the sweetener, salt, pepper, garlic powder, onion powder, and dry mustard in a small bowl and stir to combine. Sprinkle the mixture all over the brisket, then use your hands to rub it into the meat.

4.

5.   Place the brisket in the oven and cook, uncovered, for 1 hour

6.   Meanwhile, place the tomato sauce, broth and liquid smoke in a medium-sized bowl. Stir well to combine

7.   Remove the brisket from the oven and add the tomato-broth mixture to the pan. Lower the oven temperature to 300F, cover the pan, and slow cook the brisket for 2 ½ hours or until fork-tender. If the brisket isn't tender enough after 2 ½ hours, cook, covered, for an additional 30 minutes.

8.   Allow the meat to rest on a cutting board for 10 minutes while you make sauce. Pour the juices from the roasting pan into a saucepan and boil for 7 minutes or until thickened to your liking.

9.   Slice the meat across the grain into 1/8-inch slices. Serves with the sauce. Garnish with parsley, if desired.

10. Store in an airtight container in the refrigerator for up to 3 days. To reheat, place the brisket on a rimmed baking sheet in a preheated 350F oven for 5 minutes or until warmed through.

Nutritional Information: Calories 543, Carbs: 4g, Fat: 40g, Fiber: 1g, Protein: 39g

Philly Cheeses Teak Bake

Serves: 8

Preparation time: 10 minutes

Cooking time: 30 minutes

Ingredients

· 2 tablespoons olive oil, plus more for greasing the baking dish

· 1 (8-ounce) container dairy-free cream cheese (such as Kite Hill)

· ¾ cup sugar-free mayonnaise (such as Primal Kitchen)

· ¼ cup canned coconut milk or nut milk

· ¼ cup whole-grain mustard

· 2 tablespoons minced garlic

· 2 tablespoons olive oil

· 1 tomato, chopped

· 1 green bell pepper, seeded and chopped

· 1 onion, diced

· 8 ounces mushrooms, chopped

· 1½ pounds deli-sliced roast beef, chopped

Directions

1. Preheat the oven to 400°F. Grease a 9-by-13-inch baking dish.

2. In a medium bowl, stir together the cream cheese, mayonnaise, coconut milk, mustard, and garlic until well combined.

3. Heat the olive oil in a large skillet over medium heat. Add the tomato, green pepper, onion, and mushrooms. Cook, stirring frequently, until the vegetables are softened, about 8 minutes.

4. Spread the roast beef in an even layer in the prepared baking dish. Top with the vegetable mixture and then the cream cheese mixture. Bake in the preheated oven for 20 minutes, or until the dish is hot and bubbly.

Nutritional Information: Calories 534, Carbs: 5g, Fat: 42g, Fiber: 2g, Protein: 34g

Secret Seasoning Sirloin Steak

Serves: 2

Preparation time: 5 minutes

Cooking time: 20 minutes

Ingredients

·   2 (6- to 8-ounce) sirloin steaks, at room temperature

·   ¼ cup sugar-free ketchup (such as Primal Kitchen)

·   4 teaspoons garlic salt

·   ¼ cup olive oil

Directions

1.   Heat the broiler to high.

2.   Lay out the steaks on a plate and cover each side with the ketchup and garlic salt.

3.   In a cast iron skillet, heat the oil over high heat. Add the steaks and cook for 1 minute on each side.

4.   Transfer the skillet to the broiler and cook for 5 minutes more.

5.   Remove the skillet from the oven, flip the steaks over, and let them continue to cook in the hot pan for 10 more minutes.

6.   Serve immediately.

Nutritional Information: Calories 462, Carbs: 3g, Fat: 34g, Fiber: 2g, Protein: 36g

Slopy Joes

Serves: 4

Preparation time: 10 minutes

Cooking time: 30 minutes

Ingredients

- 1-pound ground beef
- 1 onion, diced
- ¾ cup sugar-free ketchup (such as Primal Kitchen)
- 2 tablespoons garlic powder
- 1 tablespoon white vinegar
- 1 tablespoon
- Swerve granular (or another granulated alternative sweetener)

Directions

1.   Heat a large skillet over medium-high heat. Add the meat and cook, stirring, until it begins to brown, about 3 minutes. Add the onion and cook, stirring frequently, until the meat is browned, and the onion is softened, about 5 minutes.

2.   Stir in the ketchup, garlic powder, vinegar, and sweetener. Reduce the heat to medium-low and cook for 20 minutes more. Serve hot.

Nutritional Information: Calories 356, Carbs: 4g, Fat: 28g, Fiber: 1g, Protein: 19g

Curry Short Ribs

Serves: 4

Preparation time: 5 minutes

Cooking time: 8 hours

Ingredients

- ¼ cup chopped onions
- ¼ cup curry powder
- 1 cup beef bone broth, homemade or store-bought
- 2 tablespoons swerve confectioners
- 1 tablespoon lime juice
- 2 cloves garlic, minced
- 4 beef short ribs (2 pounds total)

For Garnish

- Sliced scallions
- Chopped fresh cilantro

Directions

1. Place the broth, onions, curry powder, sweetener, lime juice, and garlic in a 6-quart slow cooker and stir well to combine.

2. Add the ribs and cook, covered, on a low for 7 to 8 hours or until the meat is tender and easily pulls away from the bone

3. To create a thicker, pour the sauce from the slow cooker into a saucepan and boil while whisking for 2 minutes or until thickened to your liking. Taste and add more salt or lime juice, if desired.

4. Serve the ribs with the sauce. Garnish with scallions and cilantro

5. Store in an airtight container in the refrigerator for up to 4 days. To reheat, place the ribs on a rimmed baking sheet in a preheated 400F oven for a few minutes, until warmed to your liking

Nutritional Information: Calories 528, Carbs: 4g, Fat: 47g, Fiber: 0.1g, Protein: 24g

Helen Min

Fajita Kabobs

Serves: 4

Preparation time: 10 minutes

Cooking time: 6 minutes

Ingredients

- ¼ cup lime juice
- ¼ avocado oil
- 2 cloves garlic, minced
- 1 teaspoon fine sea salt
- ¾ cayenne pepper
- 1 teaspoon chili powder
- ½ teaspoon paprika
- ½ teaspoon ground cumin
- 2 (8-ounce) boneless rib-eye steaks, about 1 inch thick
- 8 grape tomatoes
- 1 red onion
- 2 green bell peppers
- ½ cup Citrus Avocado salsa, for serving
- Boston lettuce leaves, for serving

Directions

1. Make the marinade: Place the oil, lime juice, garlic, salt, and spices in a large bowl

2. Cut the steaks into 1-inch cubes. Add the meat to marinade and stir to coat well. Cover and refrigerate for at least 1 hour or overnight

3. Preheat a grill to high heat. While the grill is heating up, cut the bell peppers and onion into 1-inch squares. Remove the meat from the marinade; reserve the marinade for basting.

4. Place 2 cubes of steak on a skewer, followed by an onion piece, a steak piece, a bell pepper piece, a steak piece, and a grape tomato, then repeat the sequence

with another piece of steak, then onion, steak, and bell pepper, ending with 2 pieces of steak. Repeat with the remaining skewers and ingredients.

5.   Lightly brush the hot grill grates with oil. Place the skewers on the grill for 3 minutes, basting every minute with the reserved marinade. Flip and cook, basting, for another 3 minutes for medium-rare steak.

6.   Serve with salsa and lettuce leaves for wrapping, if desired

7.   Store in an airtight container in the refrigerator for up to 4 days. To reheat, place in a skillet over medium heat, stirring often, for a few minutes, until warmed to your liking.

Nutritional Information: Calories 370, Carbs: 10g, Fat: 28g, Fiber: 2g, Protein: 21g

Cabbage Slaw with Ground Beef (One Pot)

Serves: 4

Preparation time: 5 minutes

Cooking time: 30 minutes

Ingredients

· 3 tablespoons olive oil

· 1-pound ground beef

· 1 (16-ounce) bag cabbage slaw mix

· 3 tablespoons coconut aminos

· 1 tablespoon fish sauce (such as Red Boat)

Directions

1. Heat the olive oil in a large skillet over medium-high heat. Add the meat and cook, stirring, until browned, about 7 minutes. Add the cabbage and cook, stirring occasionally, until wilted, about 15 minutes.

2. Stir in the coconut aminos and fish sauce, and simmer for 5 minutes more.

3. Serve hot or cover and store in the refrigerator for up to 5 days.

Nutritional Information: Calories 463, Carbs: 10g, Fat: 39g, Fiber: 1g, Protein: 18g

Cheese Burger Hash

Serves: 10

Preparation time: 20 minutes

Cooking time: 50 minutes

Ingredients

· 3 tablespoons olive oil, plus more for greasing the baking dish

· 2 pounds ground beef

· 1 (16-ounce) bag cabbage slaw mix

· 1 large onion, diced

· 8 ounces mushrooms, sliced

· 1 (8-ounce) container dairy-free cream cheese with chives (such as Kite Hill)

· 1 cup canned coconut milk

· 3 tablespoons nutritional yeast

· 2 teaspoons granulated garlic

· 1 teaspoon salt

· 1 teaspoon freshly ground black pepper

· 1 batch Perfect Bacon, crumbled

Directions

1. Preheat the oven to 350°F. Grease a 9-by-13-inch baking dish.

2. Heat the oil in a large skillet over medium-high heat. Add the meat, cabbage slaw mix, onion, and mushrooms, and cook, stirring frequently, for 15 to 20 minutes, or until the meat is browned and the vegetables are softened.

3. Transfer the mixture to the prepared baking dish.

4. In a large microwave-safe bowl, heat the cream cheese for 40 seconds in the microwave to soften.

5. To the bowl with the cream cheese, add the coconut milk, nutritional yeast, garlic, salt, and pepper, and whisk to combine well.

6. Pour the cream cheese mixture over the meat and vegetables in the baking dish. Bake in the preheated oven for 30 minutes, or until bubbling and lightly browned on top. 7Serve hot, topped with the bacon.

Nutritional Information: Calories 557, Carbs: 9g, Fat: 45g, Fiber: 4g, Protein: 29g

Kielbasa and Sauerkraut (One Pot)

Serves: 4

Preparation time: 5 minutes

Cooking time: 10 minutes

Ingredients

· 1 (16-ounce) jar or can sauerkraut

· 1-pound pork kielbasa, diced

· 2 tablespoons olive oil

Directions

1. In a medium saucepan, bring the sauerkraut to a boil over medium-high heat. Add the diced sausage and the olive oil, and simmer over low heat until heated through, about 5 minutes.

Nutritional Information: Calories 435, Carbs: 6g, Fat: 39g, Fiber: 3g, Protein: 29g

Potluck BBQ Pork

Serves: 7

Preparation time: 10 minutes

Cooking time: 8 hours

Ingredients

- 1 (2-pound) whole pork shoulder
- 2 (6-ounce) cans tomato paste
- 1 white onion, diced
- 1 cup low-carb tomato sauce
- 1 batch Red Pepper Dry Rub
- 3 tablespoons white vinegar
- 2 tablespoons coconut aminos
- 2 tablespoons whole-grain mustard

Directions

1.   In a large slow cooker, combine the pork, tomato paste, onion, tomato sauce, dry rub, vinegar, coconut aminos, and mustard.

2.   Cover and cook on low for 8 hours.

3.   Once cooked, remove the meat and shred it using a hand mixer or two forks. Return the meat to the pot and stir to mix well. Serve hot.

Nutritional Information: Calories 342, Carbs: 10g, Fat: 22g, Fiber: 4g, Protein: 29g

Garlic Pork Chops with Onion-And-Mushroom Gravy

Serves: 4

Preparation time: 10 minutes

Cooking time: 1 hour

Ingredients

- ¼ cup garlic powder
- 1 teaspoon salt
- 1 teaspoon freshly ground black pepper
- ½ teaspoon cayenne
- 4 pork chops
- ¼ cup olive oil
- 8 ounces whole mushrooms
- 1 onion, diced
- 2 cups bone broth
- ¼ cup coconut milk

Directions

1. In a small bowl, mix together the garlic powder, salt, pepper, and cayenne.

2. Coat the pork chops with the spice rub mixture, using all of the mixture.

3. Heat the oil in a large cast iron skillet over medium heat. Add the mushrooms and onion and cook, stirring frequently, until softened, about 8 minutes. Add the broth and cook for 20 minutes, or until the liquid is reduced by about half.

4. Increase the heat to high and add the pork chops. Cook for 8 to 10 minutes on each side, depending on the thickness of the pork chop, or until browned and cooked through.

5. Remove the chops from the skillet, but continue to cook the vegetables in the skillet. Add the coconut milk and cook, stirring frequently, for 2 minutes more, or until heated through and combined.

6. Serve the chops with the vegetables and gravy poured over the top.

Nutritional Information: Calories 416, Carbs: 10g, Fat: 24g, Fiber: 2g, Protein: 40g

Lemon-Garlic Pork Tenderloin with Radishes and Green Pepper

Serves: 8

Preparation time: 10 minutes

Cooking time: 8 hours

Ingredients

· 1-pound pork tenderloin

· ¼ cup olive oil

· 1 bunch of radishes (about 12), diced

· 1 green bell pepper, seeded and diced

· 1 cup bone broth

· ¾ cup Lemon-Garlic Dressing

· 4 lemon slices

Directions

1. Place the pork in a slow cooker and pour the olive oil over the top. Add the radishes and green bell pepper. Pour the broth and dressing over the top. Lay the lemon slices on top of the pork.

2. Cover and cook on low for 8 hours, or until the pork is very tender.

Nutritional Information: Calories 249, Carbs: 2g, Fat: 21g, Fiber: 0g, Protein: 13g

Citrus Pork Shoulder with Spicy Cilantro Ginger Sauce

Serves: 8

Preparation time: 10 minutes

Cooking time: 8 hours

Ingredients

· 8 cloves garlic, minced

· ¼ cup diced onions

· ¼ cup melted lard or avocado oil

· ¼ cup swerve confectioners

· 2 teaspoons ground black pepper

· 2 tablespoons fine sea salt

· 2 teaspoons smoked paprika

· Juice of 2 limes

· 4 drops orange oil

· 1 (6-pound) boneless pork shoulder

Spicy Cilantro Ginger Sauce

· ¼ cup chopped fresh cilantro

· 1 cup mayonnaise, homemade or store-bought

· ¼ cup lime juice

· 2 tablespoons chopped fresh chives

· 1 jalapeno pepper, seeded and coarsely chopped

· ½ teaspoon fine sea salt

For Garnish

· Lime wedges

· Freshly ground black pepper

Directions

1.   Place the onions, garlic, melted lard, sweetener, salt, pepper, paprika, lime juice, and orange oil in a slow cooker. Stir to combine, then place the pork shoulder on top of the other ingredients. Turn the pork in the seasonings to coat it on all sides, then cover the slow cooker and cook on low for 8 hours or until the pork shreds easily.

2.   Meanwhile, make the sauce: place all the ingredients for the sauce in a food processor and puree until very smooth. Set aside in the refrigerator until ready to serve

3.   When the meat is done, shred it with 2 forks and toss the in the juices from the slow cooker.

4.   Garnish with line wedges and freshly ground pepper.

5.   Serves each portion of meat with 3 tablespoons of the sauce.

6.   Store in an airtight container in the refrigerator for up to 3 days. To reheat, place the pork on a rimes baking sheet in a preheated 350F oven for 5 minutes or until warmed through.

Nutritional Information: Calories 712, Carbs: 3g, Fat: 59g, Fiber: 1g, Protein: 39g

Dry Rub Ribs

Serves: 8

Preparation time: 10 minutes

Cooking time: 8 hours

Ingredients

· 1 full rack baby back ribs, cut in half to fit in the pot

· 6 tablespoons olive oil

· 2 batches Red Pepper Dry Rub

· ½ cup water

Directions

1. Coat the ribs with the oil and then with the dry rub, and put them in a slow cooker with the water.

2. Cover and cook on low for 8 hours. Serve hot.

Nutritional Information: Calories 336, Carbs: 0g, Fat: 32g, Fiber: 0g, Protein: 12g

Bacon-Wrapped "Fried" Pickles

Serves: 12

Preparation time: 12 minutes

Cooking time: 25 Minutes

Ingredients

· 12 dill pickle spears

· 12 strips bacon

Directions

1. Preheat the oven to 400°F.

2. Wrap each pickle spear tightly with 1 piece of bacon.

3. Arrange the wrapped pickles on the baking sheet and bake for 25 minutes, or until the bacon is crispy.

4. Place on a wire rack to cool; the pickle juice and bacon fat make for a very hot

Nutritional Information: Calories 104, Carbs: 0g, Fat: 8g, Fiber: 0g, Protein: 7g

Stuffed Poblano Peppers

Serves: 5

Preparation time: 10 minutes

Cooking time: 40 Minutes

Ingredients

· 2 tablespoons olive oil, plus more for greasing the baking dish

· 1 pound ground pork

· 1 (4-ounce) can diced green chiles

· ½ cup tomato sauce

· 1 jalapeño pepper, chopped

· 1 tablespoon minced garlic

· 1 teaspoon dried basil

· 1 teaspoon salt

· 1 teaspoon freshly ground black pepper

· 5 poblano peppers

Directions

1. Preheat the oven to 400°F. Grease a 9-inch square baking dish.

2. In a large skillet, heat the olive oil over medium-high heat. Add the pork and begin to brown.

3. As the meat begins to brown, add the diced green chiles, tomato sauce, jalapeño, garlic, basil, salt, and pepper. Cook, stirring frequently, until the meat is browned, about 5 minutes.

4. Stuff each poblano pepper with the meat mixture, and arrange the stuffed peppers in the prepared baking dish. Bake in the preheated oven for 30 minutes, or until bubbling and browned on the top.

Nutritional Information: Calories 271, Carbs: 7g, Fat: 19g, Fiber: 2g, Protein: 18g

Shepherd's Pie (One Pot)

Serves: 10

Preparation time: 45 minutes

Cooking time: 8 hours

Ingredients

· 2 pounds ground sausage

· 1 (12-ounce) bag spinach

· 1 cup sliced mushrooms

· 1 onion, diced

· 1 cup bone broth

· ¼ cup coconut aminos

· 2 tablespoons minced garlic

· 1 recipe Cauliflower Mash, prepared but uncooked

Directions

1.   In a slow cooker, combine the sausage, spinach, mushrooms, onion, broth, coconut aminos, and garlic.

2.   Cover and cook on low for 7 hours.

3.   Spread the Cauliflower Mash over the meat mixture. Cover and cook for an additional 30 minutes to 1 hour.

4.   Serve hot.

Nutritional Information: Calories 476, Carbs: 6g, Fat: 40g, Fiber: 2g, Protein: 23g

Ground-Pork Skillet With Zucchini And Onion (One Pot)

Serves: 6

Preparation time: 10 minutes

Cooking time: 20 minutes

Ingredients

· 2 tablespoons olive oil

· 1 pound ground pork

· 1 large onion, diced

· 1 cup coconut milk

· 2 tablespoons minced garlic

· 1 teaspoon salt

· 1 teaspoon freshly ground black pepper

· 15 medium zucchini, spiralized

Directions

1. Heat the olive oil in a large skillet over medium-high heat. Add the pork and cook, stirring, until browned, about 5 minutes. Add the onion and cook, stirring frequently, until softened, about 5 more minutes.

2. Stir in the coconut milk, garlic, salt, and pepper. Reduce the heat to low and cook for about 10 more minutes, or until the sauce thickens.

3. Add the zucchini, toss to mix, and serve immediately.

Nutritional Information: Calories 329, Carbs: 5g, Fat: 29g, Fiber: 1g, Protein: 15g

Sausage Balls

Serves: 15 balls

Preparation time: 15 minutes

Cooking time: 25 minutes

Ingredients

- Oil, for greasing the baking sheet
- 1 pound loose breakfast sausage
- 2 tablespoons almond flour
- 1 tablespoon hot wing sauce (such as Frank's RedHot)
- 1 teaspoon cayenne

Directions

1. Preheat the oven to 350°F. Grease a large rimmed baking sheet.

2. In a medium bowl, thoroughly mix the breakfast sausage, almond flour, hot sauce, and cayenne. Form into bite-size balls and place on the greased baking sheet.

3. Bake for 25 minutes, or until browned and cooked through.

Nutritional Information: Calories 258, Carbs: 0g, Fat: 22g, Fiber: 0g, Protein: 15g

Chapter Eight: Desserts

No-Bake Haystack Cookies

Serves: 15 to 18 cookies

Preparation time: 10 minutes (plus 3hrs for chilling)

Ingredients

- 1 (8-ounce) container dairy-free cream cheese (such as Kite Hill)
- ¾ cup unsweetened shredded coconut
- ½ cup Swerve granular (or other granulated alternative sweetener)
- ¼ cup peanut butter
- 1 tablespoon cacao powder
- 1 tablespoon chia seeds

Directions

1. In a small microwave-safe bowl, melt the cream cheese in the microwave for 30 seconds. Whisk in the coconut, sweetener, peanut butter, cacao powder, and chia seeds.

2. On a baking sheet or plate, form the mixture into small domes, or "haystacks." Chill in the refrigerator for 3 hours (or until you've eaten them all).

Nutritional Information: Calories 172, Carbs: 5g, Fat: 16g, Fiber: 3g, Protein: 2g

Macadami Nut Butter Cups

Serves: 12 cups

Preparation time: 10 minutes (4 hours for chilling)

Ingredients

·   Coconut oil, for greasing the pan

·   1 batch Macadamia Nut Butter

·   ½ batch Chocolate Sauce

Directions

1.   Grease a silicone muffin pan with coconut oil.

2.   Pour the nut butter into the cups, dividing equally. Dampen your hands with cold water and use your fingertips to pat down and flatten the nut butter.

3.   Freeze for at least 2 hours, or until hardened.

4.   Pour the chocolate sauce over the chilled cups and freeze for at least another 2 hours, or until hardened. Serve straight from the freezer.

Nutritional Information: Calories 329, Carbs: 5g, Fat: 33g, Fiber: 1g, Protein: 3g

Peanut Butter Cookies

Serves: 15 Cookies

Preparation time: 12 minutes

Ingredients

- ¾ cup peanut butter
- 1 cup Swerve confectioners' (or another powdered alternative sweetener)
- ¼ cup olive oil
- 1 large egg

Directions

1. Preheat the oven to 325°F. Line a large baking sheet with parchment paper.

2. In a medium bowl, combine the peanut butter, sweetener, oil, and egg. Mix well.

3. Roll the batter into 1-inch balls and arrange them on the prepared baking sheet 2 inches apart. Press the tines of a fork into each cookie to get the traditional crosshatch design.

4. Bake for 12 minutes, or until lightly browned and crisp.

Nutritional Information: Calories 118, Carbs: 3g, Fat: 10g, Fiber: 1g, Protein: 4g

Best Brownies

Serves: 12

Preparation time: 10 minutes

Cook time: 25

Ingredients

- 1¼ cups Swerve granular (or another granulated alternative sweetener)
- ½ cup almond flour
- ½ cup coconut flour
- ½ cup cacao powder
- 1 teaspoon baking powder
- 1 cup olive oil
- ½ cup plus
- 2 tablespoons canned coconut milk (shake the can well before opening)
- 1 large egg
- 2 teaspoons vanilla extract

Directions

1.   Preheat the oven to 350°F.

2.   In a stand mixer, combine the sweetener, almond flour, coconut flour, cacao powder, and baking powder. With the mixer running, add the olive oil, coconut milk, egg, and vanilla extract. Mix until well combined.

3.   Fill the wells of a standard 12-cup muffin tin about halfway with the batter.

4.   Bake in the preheated oven for 25 minutes.

5.   Set the pan on a wire rack to cool completely before serving.

Nutritional Information: Calories 288, Carbs: 13g, Fat: 24g, Fiber: 8g, Protein: 5g

Lemon Squares

Serves: 9

Preparation time: 10 minutes

Cook time: 50 minutes

Ingredients

·   6 tablespoons coconut oil, melted (olive oil works fine here, too), plus more for greasing the baking dish

·   1 lemon, quartered and seeded

·   4 large eggs

·   1 cup Swerve granular (or another granulated alternative sweetener)

Directions

1.   Preheat the oven to 325°F. Grease a 9-inch square baking dish.

2.   Put the lemon wedges (including the peel) in the blender and add the eggs, sweetener, and oil. Blend until smooth.

3.   Pour the mixture into the prepared baking dish and bake for 50 minutes, or until set. Cool on a rack before cutting into squares to serve.

Nutritional Information: Calories 115, Carbs: 13g, Fat: 11g, Fiber: 0g, Protein: 3g

Pumpkin Cheese Cake

Serves: 10

Preparation time: 20 minutes

Cook time: 1 hour

Ingredients

- 6 tablespoons coconut oil, plus more for greasing the pan
- 1 cup almonds
- 1 (8-ounce) container dairy-free cream cheese (such as Kite Hill), at room temperature
- 4 large eggs
- ½ cup Swerve granular (or another granulated alternative sweetener)
- ½ cup pure pumpkin purée
- 2 teaspoons vanilla extract
- 1½ teaspoons ground cinnamon
- 1 teaspoon ground allspice
- 1 teaspoon ground ginger
- 1 teaspoon ground cloves

Directions

1. Preheat the oven to 350°F. Grease a standard 12-cup muffin tin or a 9-inch pie plate with coconut oil.

2. In a blender or food processor, combine the coconut oil and almonds, and process until finely ground.

3. Press the almond mixture into the bottom of the prepared muffin tin or pie plate and refrigerate while you make the filling.

4. In a large mixing bowl, combine the cream cheese, eggs, sweetener, pumpkin purée, vanilla extract, cinnamon, allspice, ginger, and cloves, and beat to mix well.

5. Remove the chilled crust from the refrigerator and pour in the filling mixture.

6. Bake in the preheated oven for 1 hour, or until the center is set.

Nutritional Information: Calories 246, Carbs: 5g, Fat: 22g, Fiber: 0g, Protein: 7g

Chocolate Chip Skillet Cookie

Serves: 4

Preparation time: 10 minutes

Cook time: 25 minutes

Ingredients

- Coconut oil, for greasing the skillet
- 1 cup low-carb baking mix (I like Bob's Red Mill)
- ¾ cup Swerve granular (or another granulated alternative sweetener)
- ¾ cup cacao butter, melted
- 2 teaspoons vanilla extract
- ¼ cup dairy-free chocolate chips

Directions

1. Preheat the oven to 350°F. Grease a 7-inch cast iron skillet with coconut oil.

2. In a mixing bowl, stir together the low-carb baking mix and sweetener. Add the melted cacao butter and vanilla extract and mix until well combined. Fold in the chocolate chips.

3. Pour the mixture into the greased skillet and bake for 25 minutes

Nutritional Information: Calories 415, Carbs: 4g, Fat: 43g, Fiber: 1g, Protein: 3g

Chocolate Bacon With Pink Hi-Malayan Salt (One Pot)

Serves: 4

Preparation time: 10 minutes (2 hours for Freezing)

Cook time: 25 minutes

Ingredients

· 1 batch Perfect Bacon, cooled

· ½ batch Chocolate Sauce

· 1 tablespoon pink Himalayan salt

Directions

1. Arrange the bacon on a large rimmed baking sheet and drizzle the chocolate sauce over the top.

2. Sprinkle with the salt and freeze for at least 2 hours, or until hardened.

3. Serve chilled or store in a zip-top bag in the freezer

Nutritional Information: Calories 264, Carbs: 2g, Fat: 24g, Fiber: 0g, Protein: 10g

Chocolate Chip Pie

Serves: 10

Preparation time: 20 minutes

Cook time: 40 minutes

Ingredients

For The Crust

·   2 cups almonds

·   1 cup cacao butter, melted

For The Filling

·   4 large eggs

·   ¾ cup cacao butter, melted

·   ¾ cup Swerve granular (or another granulated alternative sweetener)

·   ½ cup dairy-free chocolate chips

Directions

Making Crust

1.   Preheat the oven to 350°F.

2.   In a blender, blend the almonds and melted cacao butter. Spread the mixture out in a 9-inch pie plate. Using wet fingers, press the mixture down to spread it and smooth it out.

3.   Bake in the preheated oven for 10 minutes.

4.   Remove from the oven (but leave the oven on), and chill in the refrigerator while you make the filling.

Making The Filling

1.   In a mixing bowl, combine the eggs, cacao butter, and sweetener. Stir in the chocolate chips.

2.   Pour the batter into the chilled crust and bake for 30 minutes.

3.   Chill until set, at least 2 hours, and serve cold.

Nutritional Information: Calories 538, Carbs: 6g, Fat: 54g, Fiber: 4g, Protein: 7g

Conclusion

Thank you for purchasing a copy of this piece. I hoped it helped you enjoy a better life. I urge you to drop an honest review about the book to encourage others.

63065506R00114

Made in the USA
Columbia, SC
08 July 2019